THE ALLERGY-FREE COOK

Makes Pies and Desserts

GLUTEN-FREE, DAIRY-FREE, EGG-FREE, SOY-FREE

Laurie Sadowski

BOOK PUBLISHING COMPANY
Summertown, Tennessee

Library of Congress Cataloging-in-Publication Data

Sadowski, Laurie.
The allergy-free cook makes pies and desserts / Laurie Sadowski.
pages cm
Includes index.
ISBN 978-1-57067-308-5 (pbk.) — ISBN 978-1-57067-890-5 (e-book)
1. Gluten-free diet. 2. Gluten-free diet—Recipes. 3. Food allergy—Diet therapy—Recipes. I. Title.
RM237.86.S234 2014
641.5'638--dc23

2014018017

Pictured on the front cover: Cherry Pie with Cacao Nib Pastry Crust, p. 34

Pictured on the back cover: Cherry Pie with Cacao Nib Pastry Crust, p. 34; Shortbread Lemon Tarts with White Chocolate Drizzle, p. 72

Calculations for the nutritional analyses in this book are based on the average number of servings listed with the recipes and the average amount of an ingredient if a range is called for. Calculations are rounded up to the nearest gram. If two options for an ingredient are listed, the first one is used. Not included are optional ingredients and serving suggestions.

Cover photos: Alan Roettinger
Cover and interior design: John Wincek

Book Publishing Company
P.O. Box 99
Summertown, TN 38483
888-260-8458
bookpubco.com

ISBN: 978-1-57067-308-5

Printed in Canada

19 18 17 16 15 14 9 8 7 6 5 4 3 2 1

Book Publishing Company is a member of Green Press Initiative. We chose to print this title on paper with 100% postconsumer recycled content, processed without chlorine, which saves the following natural resources:

41 trees
1,273 pounds of solid waste
19,021 gallons of water
3,507 pounds of greenhouse gases
18 million BTU of energy

For more information on Green Press Initiative, visit greenpressinitiative.org.

Environmental impact estimates were made using the Environmental Defense Fund Paper Calculator. For more information, visit papercalculator.org.

Printed on recycled paper

Book Publishing Co.

Contents

Preface

Gluten sensitivity. Celiac disease. Food allergies. Chances are, if you've picked up this book, you or someone you know is far too familiar with these issues. The good news is that access to allergen-free, gluten-free foods is much greater than it was even just ten years ago. And I'm here to show you how to turn safe, healthful ingredients into perfect pies and decadent desserts.

I want everyone to be able to enjoy nutritious and delicious baked goods and sweet treats. When I first set out to write a book on allergen-free, gluten-free, and vegan baking, my intention was to provide people with foods they missed the most. My message remains the same today: you *can* enjoy the goodies you once loved, while accommodating restricted diets and not skimping on flavor, texture, or enjoyment.

This book is the third installment in *The Allergy-Free Cook* series. *The Allergy-Free Cook Bakes Bread* provides recipes for soft breads, gooey cinnamon buns, and crusty sandwich rolls. *The Allergy-Free Cook Bakes Cakes and Cookies* delivers cakes of all kinds, fudgy brownies and bars, and cookies galore. This volume rounds out the dessert spectrum with pies, cobblers, ice cream, trifles, and just about everything in between.

Like the others in the series, this book meets the needs of those who consume a gluten-free diet. The recipes are also vegan and suitable for people who do not eat dairy products or eggs. In addition, none of the recipes call for nightshades or soy, which can trigger food allergies or sensitivities. And finally, any recipes that contain legumes, nuts, peanuts, seeds, and yeast are clearly marked so you can modify those recipes if you need to.

Health and nutrition are priorities for me, but let's be honest—so is dessert. If you feel the same, you've found the best of both worlds in this book. And in me, you've found a kindred spirit.

So . . . when can I come over for dessert?

Laurie Sadowski

Acknowledgments

It's no secret I love food, and that love has launched me into a great adventure that I have shared with many amazing people. I certainly couldn't have produced a series of cookbooks without the support of my publisher and some other serious food lovers. Much thanks goes to Book Publishing Company for being incredible in every way imaginable. Jo and Cynthia, I appreciate your constant input and advice, and Bob and Anna, you're fabulous people.

I also want to give a big thank-you to the following: To my parents, who have had to accept that I bring them dessert every day. To Emerald and Lydia, I couldn't have done this one without you. To Xavi and Gretchen, for listening to my constant barrage of recipe ideas. To Andrea, Anja, Becky, Brenda, Carolynn, Claire, Courtney, Jordanna, Keri, Kerri, Leigh, Lidia, Mat, Shelda, Shiona, Stasia, Tiffany, and Tina for all your feedback.

And to my running shoes . . . because without you, I'd never be able to eat everything I bake.

Introduction

Sure, I was in the kitchen growing up. Mixing muffins alongside Mom. Preparing pierogi and caramel corn with my grandmas. Making chocolate chip cookies for fueling late-night study sessions.

But it wasn't until 2005, when I was first diagnosed with celiac disease, that I got serious in the kitchen. I had to be serious. The illness had left me dehydrated, weak, and weighing far less than I should.

I felt better immediately after adopting a strict gluten-free diet. However, it quickly became clear that my new diet didn't fix all my health problems; I soon realized that casein, a milk protein, was creating neurological symptoms, chest tightness, and a mysterious rash. In addition to leaving gluten behind, I cut out all forms of dairy. By avoiding both, I found the way to recover my health.

The kitchen became my second home, and I decided to write a cookbook with the hope that I could help other people who also faced illness caused by particular foods. I self-published *Mission in the Kitchen*, a book that exclusively featured gluten-free and casein-free recipes. I sold more copies of the book than I ever anticipated.

Around the same time, I started looking at all my food choices in a new light. Because plant-based foods were easy to digest, I incorporated them more and more into my meals. I developed a distaste for meat and eggs. And having already eliminated dairy products, I became a vegan.

This evolution, and my newfound love for baking, led to more writing. My passion was gluten-free and vegan baked goods. My enthusiasm encompassed an endless variety of healthful creations, from breads to ice cream to cookies. I wanted to write about everything I missed and longed to enjoy again. But there was one problem: I had too many ideas for just one book.

And so came *The Allergy-Free Cook* series, which features all the recipes of my dreams and so much more. I provide the basics about gluten, food allergies, and food sensitivities. Plus, I help you rethink your baking strategy and restock your pantry with whole foods and wholesome ingredients . . . stuff that tastes amazing and is good for us too.

I strongly believe we must nourish our bodies for them to thrive. After all, good health is the best gift we can give ourselves. For people with celiac disease, gluten sensitivity, and food allergies, nourishing the body can be especially tricky. These challenges require us to look at food a different way, to break from old-school traditions and routines, and actively investigate a new world of products and information that is now readily in reach.

We all deserve dessert, and now, if we're willing to make some modifications, we can all have it. So let's get started. Pie à la mode, anyone?

Coca-Cola
Kropla

PART I

Gluten Sensitivity and Food Allergies

A wise man should consider that health is the greatest of human blessings, and learn how by his own thought to derive benefit from his illnesses.

HIPPOCRATES

Did you ever watch a house being built? Early on, the frame goes up, and it's the frame that provides structure and holds the house together. In conventional baking, gluten functions like the frame.

Gluten is a protein—a building block—found in wheat, rye, and barley that helps bind baked goods together. The word "gluten" literally means "glue." Without gluten or an effective substitute, baked goods can fall apart and be dry and crumbly. But fear not: this book is full of information about effective gluten substitutes that provide texture and structure that rival any gluten-filled baked good.

There are different reasons to avoid gluten. People with celiac disease, like me, must follow a strict, gluten-free diet for life. Celiac disease is an autoimmune disorder that interferes with the small intestine's ability to absorb nutrients. It also causes gastrointestinal problems, neurological issues, and fatigue. Untreated, it can result in weight loss, nutritional deficiencies, skin disorders, and a host of other symptoms. It's estimated that 1 in 133

Americans have celiac disease, and people who seek help for their symptoms often face a long road to diagnosis.

Other people who have difficulty digesting gluten have what's known as gluten sensitivity, which, unlike celiac disease, isn't an autoimmune response but can result in similar symptoms. Furthermore, research has shown that people with arthritis, Crohn's disease, diabetes, fibromyalgia, irritable bowel syndrome, multiple sclerosis, and ulcerative colitis may also benefit from a gluten-free diet.

If gluten is a problem for you or members of your household, learning how to bake without gluten heralds a new day—or at least a new dessert (or two!). If you're a seasoned baker, gluten-free baking requires you to rethink the way you bake; in fact, baking novices may have the advantage here precisely because they're not accustomed to working with all-purpose wheat flour. In gluten-free baking, there are more than twenty flours to choose from; moreover, in my recipes, one single flour simply won't cut it! Mixing and matching flours is key to getting just the right taste and texture. The days of having only one flour in your pantry are gone. With gluten-free baking, you'll find that your choices aren't limited; rather, it opens up a whole world of options.

In this book, most recipes call for sorghum, quinoa, teff, and millet flours. When you become familiar with these flours, you'll quickly see how they outshine all-purpose wheat flour—and not just in taste. The bonus is that most gluten-free flours are nutritionally superior to wheat flour. And as you become adept in this new style of baking and take your own needs and preferences into consideration, you can expand your repertoire to incorporate many other types of flours. Details about gluten-free flours, starches, and other ingredients are provided in Part II (see page 7).

The recipes in this book are free not only of gluten but also of other problematic ingredients. Because it's common for people with celiac disease or food allergies to have multiple food sensitivities, I clearly indicate which common allergens are absent from each recipe.

OTHER FOOD ALLERGIES AND SENSITIVITIES

True food allergies are caused by proteins in certain foods. The immune system inaccurately perceives these proteins as enemies, which causes an adverse immune response. When the immune system rallies to the body's defense, mild to severe allergic reactions occur. These can range from hives to trouble breathing and even loss of consciousness.

Food intolerances or sensitivities, while potentially less severe than food allergies, also cause negative reactions. A food intolerance can occur, for example, in someone who lacks a specific digestive enzyme. Lactose intolerance, or the inability to adequately digest the milk sugar lactose, occurs in about 30 million Americans and triggers gastrointestinal and respiratory issues. People who are newly diagnosed with celiac disease often experience temporary lactose intolerance, because their damaged intestines cannot absorb lactose properly.

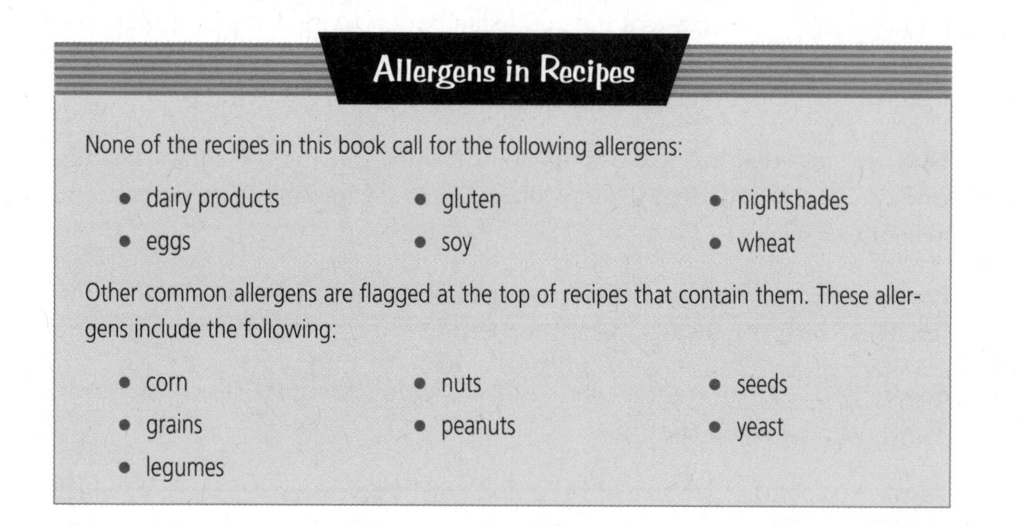

Allergens in Recipes

None of the recipes in this book call for the following allergens:

- dairy products
- gluten
- nightshades
- eggs
- soy
- wheat

Other common allergens are flagged at the top of recipes that contain them. These allergens include the following:

- corn
- nuts
- seeds
- grains
- peanuts
- yeast
- legumes

Check the Allergen Information for Each Recipe

Because all the recipes in this book are vegan, they contain no animal-based ingredients. This means that dairy products and eggs will not be found in this book. Of course, gluten and wheat are also avoided. In addition, soy and nightshades, such as potato starch, are not used in any of the recipes.

Even without animal-based products, gluten, wheat, soy, and nightshades, some of the recipes in this book may include ingredients that trigger allergic reactions in some people. That's why, as you look through this book, you'll notice that immediately below each recipe title is a list of common allergens. Corn, grains, legumes, nuts, peanuts, seeds, and yeast are all flagged in the recipes that call for these ingredients.

Here is information about items that may be listed in the allergen information for each recipe:

Corn. Recipes that are free of corn don't include cornmeal or cornstarch. They also don't call for baking powder or xanthan gum, which contain corn derivatives, and vegan buttery spread, which has natural flavor derived from corn.

Grains. Recipes that are free of grains don't include any grains or pseudograins, such as quinoa or teff, which are seeds. They also don't include baking powder, xanthan gum, or flours and starches made from corn or tapioca.

Legumes. Recipes that are free of legumes don't include bean-based flours and peanuts (which are legumes, not nuts). Earth Balance soy-free vegan buttery spread, which I recommend for those who can safely use it, contains legumes (pea protein), so recipes that include vegan buttery spread aren't legume-free. Similarly, canned coconut milk often contains guar gum, which is made from legumes, so recipes that include coconut milk aren't legume-free.

Nuts. Recipes that are free of nuts don't include tree nuts, such as almonds, cashews, hazelnuts, pecans, and walnuts. These recipes may include coconut, peanuts, or seeds.

Peanuts. Recipes that are free of peanuts don't include peanuts or peanut butter. These recipes may include nuts or seeds.

Seeds. Recipes that are free of seeds don't include chia, flax, or other seeds. These recipes may include nuts.

Yeast. Recipes that are free of yeast don't include yeast; cider vinegar, which is a fermented food; or vegan buttermilk, which is made with vinegar.

Interpret Food Labels Carefully

Food labels can be deceptive. Despite new labeling laws and government guidelines, allergens (including many with unfamiliar names) can still be found in packaged goods. Table 1 (page 5) outlines words for hidden ingredients in packaged foods that may include gluten, dairy, egg, or soy products.

Some packaged foods are essential in baking, and it's important to always read ingredient lists when shopping or before using new products at home. In addition, scrutinize each product label to learn what you can about the manufacturer's practices. Gluten-free flour, for example, may appear to be safe, but it's not if it's made on the same equipment as wheat flour. If you're unsure about a manufacturer or product, all it takes is a phone call (see step 5, page 6).

Seven Steps for Getting Started

Are you ready to get started on a new adventure in baking? The destination is great taste and good health. Before you begin, I recommend you browse

TABLE 1 Common terms for items containing gluten, dairy, egg, or soy products

Ingredient	Words to look for
Wheat	Bran, bread flour, brown flour, bulgur, durum, enriched flour, farina, faro, germ, gluten, graham, groats, hydrolyzed wheat protein, Kamut, roux, seitan, semolina, spelt, triticum, udon (wheat noodles), wheat starch
Barley	Barley grass, barley groats, barley malt, barley syrup, beer, brown rice syrup (could contain barley), malt, pearl barley
Dairy/casein	All dairy products, artificial butter flavor, butter, butter oil, butterfat, casein, caseinates (ammonia, calcium, magnesium, potassium, sodium), custard, ghee, goat's milk, hydrolysates, kefir, lactalbumin phosphate, lactate, lactic acid, lactoglobulin, lactose, lactulose, margarine, milk fat, milk protein, milk solids, nougat, pudding, rennet, sherbet, spread, whey
Eggs	Albumin, binder, coagulant, eggs (powdered, white, whole, yolk, or yellow), emulsifier, lecithin, livetin, lysozyme, ovalbumin, ovamucin, ovamucoid, ovovitellin, vitellin
Soy	Hydrolyzed or textured (plant, soy, and vegetable) protein, lecithin, monodiglycerides, monosodium glutamate, natto, okara, soja, soy protein concentrate or isolate, vegetable oil, vegetable protein, yuba
Other	Artificial flavors, avena (oats), bread, breading, cereal, chocolate, couscous, croutons, imitation bacon, oatmeal, oats, rye, starch

through the recipes (but if you've got a sweet tooth like mine, I bet you've already done that!). Then consider the following seven steps, which will help you achieve the best results.

1. Restock the pantry. If you've baked with wheat flour in the past, it's possible your baking supplies are contaminated with gluten. For example, cross-contamination likely occurred if you used the same measuring spoon to dip into different ingredients, including those that contained gluten. So ditch open containers of baking powder, spices, and other leftover items that may no longer be safe.

2. Check your baking gear. Crumbs and other minuscule food remnants can lurk in kitchen equipment, such as blenders, sifters, and stand mixers. Specifically, cutting boards, nonstick bakeware, and wooden spoons can be porous and harbor contaminants. Clean or replace items as necessary.

3. Choose your recipes. Start with something simple or familiar. If you're an apple aficionado, try Maple-Apple-Pecan Crisp (page 91)—it's super easy. If you're pastry proficient, opt for Peach Pie with Buttery Double Crust (page 32).

4. Practice safe shopping habits. This means reading labels, of course, but it also means sidestepping the bulk bins, where even gluten-free ingredients might be contaminated. Many shoppers might not think twice about using the scoop for the barley inside the bin for the sorghum flour, for example. In addition, avoid bulk nuts and dried fruit, which may be dusted with wheat flour to discourage sticking.

5. Call some companies. If you're unsure about the contents or safety of any product, call the manufacturer. Ask about gluten and allergens that may be present in a specific product or other items that are produced on the same equipment or in the same plant. Responsible companies will be happy to share their strategies for avoiding cross-contamination.

6. Start baking. Take your time. Have all of the ingredients and measuring gear ready to go before you begin a recipe. This step is especially important for a recipe, such as a pie or a trifle, that has many steps.

7. Store ingredients safely. This step can be very helpful if you live in a shared household that is not gluten-free. Set aside an area exclusively for gluten-free goods. Store gluten-containing and gluten-free baking ingredients in sealed containers in separate cabinets, and label condiments to avoid cross-contamination.

PART II

Gluten-Free Ingredients and Tips for Success

The only real stumbling block is fear of failure. In cooking you've got to have a what-the-hell attitude.

JULIA CHILD

Dessert lovers. You know who you are. No matter how delicious the meal, you've reserved loosening your belt buckle for the pie, cheesecake, tart, cobbler, pudding, or ice cream to come. As far as you're concerned, having this sweet treat at the end of the meal is, in fact, saving the best for last. Of course, to make desserts that are worth looking forward to, you must start with the best ingredients. Whether you're letting your creative juices flow, experimenting with new flavors to make your taste buds sing, or replicating a classic just like Grandma used to make, pick your ingredients carefully. For me, that means turning to my gluten-free faves.

PACK YOUR PANTRY: GLUTEN-FREE FLOURS AND STARCHES

To mimic the results of using wheat flour, I combine different gluten free flours and add xanthan gum or guar gum (see page 10) to provide structure. Many gluten-free flours are available, and I have experimented with them to accommodate my own tastes and needs. In the process, I've happily discovered that gluten-free baking can trump wheat-based baking not only in taste but also in nutrition!

It's best to create a flour combination for each recipe. I avoid using all-purpose gluten-free mixes from the store because these may include refined ingredients, dry milk, and gelatin—and none of these correspond with my lifestyle or dietary restrictions. In addition, I offer no "master flour mix" that can be plugged into each recipe. While some people might prefer this one-size-fits-all approach, my passion for recipe development is fueled by the unique taste and texture of gluten-free flours. I recommend a variety of combinations because I know some flours perform certain tasks better than others. The key here is discovering the properties and flavor of each flour. That's why this section goes into detail about key ingredients.

I encourage you to follow my recipes as written, but if you *must* change an ingredient, you can use table 2, page 11, to substitute your own gluten-free flour combinations. And remember, the key to kitchen success is starting with high-quality ingredients and experimenting.

Essential Flours and Starches

Let's start with the list of gluten-free flours I use in this book:

Sorghum flour. Sorghum flour has a neutral flavor, a great texture, and an admirable nutritional profile. In addition, its low cost makes it an affordable choice. I tend to use it for at least half the total amount of flour in my flour combinations.

Quinoa flour. Rich in fiber, iron, and protein, quinoa flour adds structure to gluten-free recipes. Because of its strong flavor, I recommend using quinoa flour for no more than one-quarter of the total amount of flour in any flour combination.

Teff flour. High in protein, slightly sweet, and somewhat nutty, teff flour has similar nutritional properties to quinoa flour. It's also a pleasant complement to cocoa or molasses.

Millet flour. Rich in B vitamins, millet flour is somewhat sweet and adds a moist, tender crumb to baked goods. This makes it an especially good flour to use when baking cakes, such as the pudding cakes and trifles in this book.

Cornmeal. Cornmeal is available in white, yellow, and blue. A key ingredient in cornbread and polenta, it provides a dense, crumbly texture.

The two starches used in this book are arrowroot starch and tapioca flour, which also work well as thickeners. I don't use cornstarch, because most brands, like most processed corn products, are genetically modified. I also avoid potato starch to keep recipes free of nightshades.

Arrowroot starch. Also known as arrowroot flour, arrowroot starch adds body and texture and works as a binding agent.

Tapioca flour. Also known as tapioca starch, tapioca flour is made from the cassava plant. It adds moistness and gives baked goods a tender, chewy texture.

Optional Flours and Starches

In addition to my favorites listed above, many other flours and starches can be used in gluten-free baking. However, none of the following items are used in this book.

Amaranth flour. Amaranth flour is high in protein, adds structure to baked goods, and has a nutty and peppery taste.

Buckwheat flour. Buckwheat flour has a distinct earthy flavor, is rich in nutrients, and is best known for its use in pancakes.

Chickpea flour. Chickpea flour is high in fiber and protein and adds moisture to baked goods. However, some people don't care for its strong taste.

Coconut flour. Coconut flour is high in fat and fiber. In fact, because of its high fiber content, it readily absorbs wet ingredients. Therefore, be sure to proportionally increase the amount of liquid if using coconut flour to convert a conventional recipe.

Cornstarch. Cornstarch is the powdery substance inside of the corn kernel. It is often used as a thickening agent or as a substitute for another starch.

Garfava flour. Garfava flour combines chickpea (or garbanzo bean) and fava bean flours and has a less distinct taste than either of these flours alone. It is high in protein and adds structure to baked goods.

Nut flours. Also known as nut meals, nut flours are high in fiber and fat. They add moisture, flavor, and texture to baked goods. Almond and hazelnut flours are the most common.

Oat flour. Oats are safe only if produced by a company specializing in certified gluten-free oats. People with celiac disease should check with their health care providers before including oats in their diets.

Potato starch. Potato starch is also known as potato starch flour, but it isn't the same as potato flour. Potato starch is very fine and, like other starches, works well as a thickener and adds moisture to baked goods.

Rice flour. There are three main types of rice flour: white, brown, and sweet. Both white and brown rice flours have a gritty texture; in addition, brown rice flour has a hint of nuttiness. Sweet rice flour is also called "glutinous rice flour," which is gluten-free (here, "glutinous" refers not to gluten but to the sticky texture of the rice). Sweet rice flour is similar to starches and works well as a thickener.

Flours and Starch Substitutions

There are many reasons to opt for alternative flours and starches when baking. For example, you may want to switch things up because of a specific food intolerance or to accommodate your own tastes. Or you may simply want to use the items in your pantry instead of waiting to buy something you don't have in stock. Whatever your reason, you should find table 2 (page 11) helpful. Table 2 lists a variety of flours, including wheat flour, and starches. The table includes wheat flour so you can refer to it when adapting your favorite wheat-based recipes.

When substituting, choose flours with similar weight, fiber, and protein contents for the best results. For example, if a recipe calls for quinoa flour, try almond flour instead because it has a similar protein and fiber content. Ideally, the interchanged flours should have the same weight per cup.

Like wheat flour, some gluten-free flours, such as chickpea flour, coconut flour, cornmeal, and nut flours, can be used alone. Others should be used in combination. To create your own gluten-free flour combo, try the following guideline: use a neutral flour to make up 50 percent of the mix, use a flour that is higher in protein to make up 25 percent of the mix, and use a starch to make up the other 25 percent. And don't forget the xanthan gum (see below for details).

Xanthan Gum

If you're new to gluten-free baking, xanthan gum may be new to you, but it's role is really quite simple. Xanthan gum helps bind gluten-free baked goods and is an excellent substitute for gluten. However, an equal amount of guar gum can replace xanthan gum in most instances.

Although the amount of xanthan gum needed can vary per recipe, a good general rule for most desserts is ½ teaspoon of xanthan gum per 1 cup of gluten-

TABLE 2 Properties of flours and starches

Flour (¼ cup)	Calories, kcal	Fat, grams	Fiber, grams	Protein, grams	Weight, grams	Properties*
Almond flour	160	14	3	6	28	N, O, P
Amaranth flour	110	2	3	4	30	N, P
Arrowroot starch	110	0	1	0	32	S
Buckwheat flour	100	1	4	4	30	P
Chickpea flour	110	2	5	6	30	P, O
Coconut flour	120	3	12	4	28	O
Cornmeal	110	1	5	2	32	O
Cornstarch	120	0	0	0	32	S
Fava bean flour	110	0.5	8	9	33	P
Garfava flour	150	2.5	3	9	30	P
Hazelnut flour	180	17	3	4	28	N, O, P
Millet flour	110	1	4	3	30	N, P
Potato starch	160	0	0	0	48	S
Quinoa flour	120	2	4	4	28	P
Rice flour, brown	140	1	2	3	39.5	N
Rice flour, sweet white	180	0.5	1	3	51	S
Rice flour, white	150	0.5	1	2	39.5	N
Sorghum flour	120	1	3	4	31.75	N
Tapioca flour	100	0	0	0	30	S
Teff flour	113	1	4	4	30	P
Wheat flour (all-purpose)	120	1	1	4	34	O
Wheat flour (whole wheat)	110	0.5	4	4	33	O

***Properties:** N = neutral flours, P = higher-protein flours, O = flours that can be used on their own, S = starch

free flour. When experimenting, remember that too little xanthan gum may result in a crumbly texture, while too much will make baked goods gummy.

Leaveners

Leaveners, such as baking powder, baking soda, and cider vinegar, help baked goods rise and stay moist. Leaveners also influence the texture of baked goods. Using fresh baking powder and baking soda is a must (see sidebar, page 12).

Baking powder. Baking powder is a chemical leavener that helps batters rise and, in eggless baking, also assists in binding the ingredients. Using too much baking powder can cause a bitter taste or make baked goods collapse; using too little may inhibit rising or make baked goods tough. Baking powder contains cornstarch. If you're allergic to or sensitive to corn, replace each teaspoon of baking powder with the following combination: ½ teaspoon of cream of tartar and 1 teaspoon of baking soda.

Baking soda. Also known as sodium bicarbonate, baking soda is a chemical leavener that is about four times stronger than baking powder. It's used in recipes that contain an acid, such as citrus juice, molasses, vegan buttermilk (see sidebar, page 23), or vinegar. Baking soda begins to react as soon as it's mixed with wet ingredients, so be sure to bake items containing baking soda immediately after mixing. Using too much baking soda will result in a coarse, dry crumb or soapy taste.

Cider vinegar. Also known as apple cider vinegar, cider vinegar adds tenderness and lift to gluten-free and egg-free baked goods. It also can be combined with nondairy milk to make vegan buttermilk (see sidebar, page 23).

The Fresh Test: Baking Powder and Baking Soda

For the best results, test leaveners for freshness before using.

- Mix 1 teaspoon of baking powder with ½ cup of hot water. If the mixture bubbles immediately, the baking powder is fresh.
- Mix ¼ teaspoon of baking soda with 2 teaspoons of vinegar. If the mixture bubbles immediately, the baking soda is fresh.

PART III

Additional Ingredients and Smart Substitutions

There is no love sincerer than the love of food.

GEORGE BERNARD SHAW

Desserts are sweet indulgences, and they're even better when they're allergy friendly and contain high-quality ingredients. And trust me, you'll have no trouble persuading your family and friends to have a second Deep-Dish Chocolate Chip Cookie Bowls (page 105)!

UNREFINED SWEETENERS

To make dessert, you have to use a little sweetener. Sometimes, very nutritious ingredients, such as dates (see page 14) or other fruits, can put the "sweet" in your treats. Other times, the best choice is a minimally processed sweetener that has no added ingredients. Here are some of the sweeteners used in this book.

Agave nectar. Agave nectar is a liquid sweetener that's naturally sweeter than sugar. Thanks to its low-glycemic index, it's absorbed into the body more slowly than sugar and is less likely to cause a spike in blood sugar levels. Agave nectar is neutral in flavor and available in light, amber, and raw varieties. Because baked goods made with agave nectar tend to brown quickly, it's important to make adjustments when using agave nectar as a substitute for other sweeteners: for the best results, decrease the oven temperature by 25 degrees F and increase the baking time by 5 to 10 minutes.

Confectioners' sugar. Also known as powdered sugar or icing sugar, confectioners' sugar is a granulated sugar that has been ground to a powder and combined with cornstarch to prevent clumping or crystallization. I use it minimally, often in glazes and frostings, since it's refined. Check the label before purchasing: some brands are ground with wheat starch.

Dates. Fiber-rich dates are all natural and an excellent source of sweetness. I recommend honey dates for the best flavor and texture. If the dates you have are firm or dry, soak them in warm water for 10 minutes to make them tender before using. Check the label before purchasing: dates might be dusted with flour to prevent sticking.

Molasses. Molasses is a thick syrup that's separated from raw cane sugar during the sugar-making process. There are different varieties of molasses. Light molasses is light in flavor and color; dark molasses has a deeper flavor and color; and blackstrap molasses has the most intense flavor.

Pure maple syrup. Pure maple syrup comes from the sap of maple trees and shouldn't be confused with pancake syrup. There are two broad classifications of maple syrup: grade A (also called "light") and grade B (also called "amber"). I recommend grade B for its stronger maple flavor.

Unrefined cane sugar. Unrefined cane sugar is minimally processed, meaning minerals, trace elements, and vitamins are left intact. Imparting the same sweetness as refined sugar, unrefined cane sugar has a hint of molasses flavor that adds depth to baked goods. I recommend Sucanat brand, which is made by Wholesome Sweeteners.

Other common sweeteners include granulated white sugar, brown sugar, Demerara sugar, and brown rice syrup. If you use any of these sweeteners in place of the recommended sweetener in my recipes, your results may vary.

Sweet Substitutions

To use a liquid sweetener in place of a granulated sweetener, use ⅔ cup of liquid sweetener for every cup of granulated sweetener and decrease the total amount of other liquids in the recipe by 2 tablespoons. When using agave nectar, decrease the oven temperature by 25 degrees F and increase the baking time by 5 to 10 minutes.

GOOD-FOR-YOU FATS

Fat plays a vital role in baking, producing flaky, melt-in-your-mouth pastries, biscuit toppings, and silky ice creams. Healthful fats also provide important nutrients. Here are the good-for-you fats I prefer for baking and dessert making.

Vegan buttery spread. Vegan buttery spread can be used measure for measure to replace butter in any recipe. Earth Balance brand is nonhydrogenated and free of trans fats and, for those with sensitivities, even comes in a soy-free version. I recommend this product over any other option because it works beautifully in baked goods (better than dairy-free margarines) and is widely available. Note that the soy-free version of Earth Balance includes legumes (pea protein).

Buttery-tasting vegan spread is essential when a buttery flavor is desired, especially when making pastry. If you don't have vegan buttery spread on hand or want to try an oil-based pastry crust, see page 30 for tips on using coconut oil instead.

Coconut oil. Coconut oil is a nonhydrogenated source of health-promoting saturated fats. There are two kinds: unrefined (or virgin) and refined (or simply not labeled virgin). Virgin coconut oil has the distinct scent and flavor of coconut and costs about twice as much as the refined variety; both, however, are nutritionally the same. Look for a high-quality brand of refined coconut oil for all-purpose use.

Coconut oil is liquid when warmed, rock solid when refrigerated, and the texture of softened butter at room temperature (unless your house is very warm). If a recipe calls for softened coconut oil, it should be scoopable but not melted.

Avocado. Mashed avocado flesh can sometimes be used in place of fat and eggs (see table 3, page 22). It has buttery undertones and can often replace heavy cream or cream cheese, adding silkiness to frostings and mousses.

Other oils, such as canola, grapeseed, and olive oils, can be used for baking. It isn't always possible to use these oils in place of coconut oil, since coconut oil is solid at room temperature.

NUTS, SEEDS, PEANUTS, AND COCONUT

Nuts, seeds, peanuts, and coconut provide texture and add nutrients to baked goods. If you have allergies, you can omit or replace these ingredients, and the recipe will typically turn out just fine. For extra flavor, toast the nuts, seeds, or coconut before using (see sidebar, page 16).

If you're not accustomed to using seeds when making desserts, it's time to discover how these tiny contributors can take your efforts to the next level. Chia seeds and flaxseeds, which are often classified as superfoods, are excellent sources of essential omega-3 fatty acids and other nutrients and phytochemicals. Flaxseeds should be ground before using; grind flaxseeds in a coffee grinder reserved for that purpose or purchase them in ground form (ground flaxseeds may be labeled "flax meal" or "flaxseed meal"). Both chia seeds and flax seeds make excellent egg replacements (see table 3, page 22), and both should be stored in the refrigerator.

Toasting Nuts, Seeds, and Coconut

To toast them in the oven, spread the nuts, seeds, or coconut in a single layer on a baking sheet. Preheat the oven to 400 degrees F and bake for 3 to 4 minutes. Stir thoroughly, then bake for 3 to 4 minutes longer, until golden.

To toast them in a skillet, spread the nuts, seeds, or coconut in a single layer. Cook over medium-high heat, stirring often, until fragrant and golden, 5 to 7 minutes.

These items burn quickly, so remove them from the baking sheet or pan immediately after toasting. Let cool completely before using.

Peanut, nut, seed, and coconut butters make delicious and creamy additions to baked goods. When purchasing, look for natural varieties, with the only ingredient being the nut itself. Roasted varieties are more flavorful, while raw versions are more subtle in taste. When opening a new jar of nut butter, stir in the natural oil that separates out and rises to the top; otherwise, the nut butter won't be creamy or as effective in baking.

Making Homemade Nut and Seed Butters

To make your own nut or seed butter, put about 3 cups of nuts or seeds (raw or toasted) in a heavy-duty food processor fitted with the metal S blade. Process until completely smooth, about 15 minutes, stopping occasionally to scrape down the work bowl if necessary. If you're having trouble getting a completely smooth finish, add 1 tablespoon of a nut-based or neutral oil.

Use the same method for making coconut butter, using about 4 cups of unsweetened finely shredded dried coconut. Coconut butter will be very runny when first processed but will become firm as it stands; it's usually ready to use about 3 hours after processing.

When it comes to coconut flakes, use unsweetened finely shredded dried coconut for the best results. Let's Do Organic... by Edward & Sons makes an allergy-friendly option.

FRESH FRUIT

Many recipes in this book highlight fruit as a main ingredient, and using fruit in your desserts is one wonderful way to take advantage of its abundance during the peak season. In fact, having grown up around fruit farms, I know just how essential the quality of the fruit is to the outcome of the dessert. By opting for the freshest, and preferably local, ingredients, you can often decrease the sugar and let the fruits fully shine.

Apples. Apples should be aromatic, colorful, smooth, shiny, and have no soft spots. My favorite baking apple is Mutsu (also known as Crispin), a sweet-tart variety that holds its shape and grows abundantly where I live. In addition, apples such as Cortland, Fuji, Golden Delicious, Gravenstein, Northern Spy, and Pink Lady are good choices for baking. Tart varieties, such as Granny Smith, can be used in baking, but additional sweetener may be needed to compensate for their tartness. Other common varieties, such as McIntosh, are best for applesauce, while Red Delicious is not recommended for baking or cooking.

Avocados. Ripe avocados have dark skin and yield to firm, gentle pressure. Very soft avocados are overripe. Because avocados ripen at room temperature, storing them in the refrigerator slows the ripening process. Use ripe avocados within one day.

Cherries. Cherries should be plump, bright in color, wrinkle-free, and have green stems. They don't ripen after they're picked, so use them soon after purchasing.

Citrus fruits. Citrus fruits, including lemons, limes, oranges, and grapefruits, should be plump and have smooth, tight skin and fine pores. Color doesn't indicate flavor.

Cranberries. Cranberries should be deep red, shiny, and not shriveled. They should be firm to the touch and bounce if dropped on the counter or table. Unlike most fruits, cranberries freeze well, with no change in texture or flavor.

Currants (red). Currants should be plump, bright in color, and wrinkle-free. Avoid wrinkled currants or currants with brown stems.

Peaches, plums, nectarines, apricots. Peaches, plums, nectarines, and apricots should be smooth, unblemished, and wrinkle-free. Color doesn't indicate taste or texture, and heavier fruits are juicier. These fruits should yield slightly to the touch when ripe; they ripen at room temperature and ripen more quickly when stored in a paper bag. Refrigerate once they are ripe.

Pears. Pears should be bright in color and free of any soft spots. They should yield to gentle pressure when squeezed, and they ripen at room temperature. When baking, choose varieties such as Bartlett and Comice.

Persimmons (fuyu). Fuyu persimmons should be bright in color and free of bruises or blemishes. When used for baking, they should yield to gentle pressure when squeezed. Don't confuse fuyu persimmons with hachiya persimmons, which have a mousse-like texture, must be very ripe for consumption, and can't be substituted for the fuyu variety.

Pineapples. Pineapples should have green leaves, not brown or wilted leaves, a strong pineapple scent, and a firm shell. The exterior color doesn't indicate ripeness; even green pineapples can be ripe.

Raspberries, blackberries, boysenberries, blueberries. All of these berries should be plump, wrinkle-free, and shiny, and blueberries should be a deep purple-blue (not reddish). Because they have a short shelf life, use berries as soon as possible after picking or purchasing. Don't wash berries until right before using.

Rhubarb. Rhubarb stalks should look swollen and glossy. Thin stalks lack flavor and thick ones are very fibrous. Color doesn't indicate ripeness or flavor. Note that rhubarb leaves are poisonous, so remove them before using the fruit.

Strawberries. Strawberries should be plump, with a natural shine and a rich red color. The caps should be bright green. Strawberries don't ripen after they're picked, so use them as soon as possible after picking or purchasing.

Frozen Fruit versus Fresh

If a recipe calls for fresh fruit and you use frozen fruit instead, the finished product might turn out quite differently than it would have if you had used fresh. The texture, in particular, is likely to be affected, because frozen fruits typically contain more liquid than fresh fruits (although some can actually be drier than fresh fruits if they aren't sufficiently ripe). Generally, using frozen fruit means a recipe will require a longer baking time because frozen fruit lowers the internal temperature of the batter, which means it will take longer to cook. Sometimes, drained defrosted fruit is acceptable. For the best results, however, use what is listed in the recipe.

FLAVOR ENHANCERS

When baking, it's essential to get the right balance of wet and dry ingredients. However, there are many flavor enhancers that can be added to or substituted in a recipe without affecting this delicate ratio. Here are just a few examples of flavoring agents that can add oomph to desserts.

Citrus. Finely grated citrus zest highlights other ingredients without overpowering their taste. Citrus juice can replace part of the liquid ingredients to provide a different flavor. Lemon juice, in particular, can brighten the flavor and retard the discoloration of other fruits.

Extracts. Vanilla extract is a popular ingredient, but other extracts, such as almond, chocolate, hazelnut, maple, mint, orange, and rum, can add versatility to any recipe. Extracts can also mask the strong taste of some gluten-free flours.

Salt. In baking, salt generally isn't used to add a salty flavor. Instead, it's used to slow chemical reactions, promote a steady rate of baking, add structure to batters and doughs, and increase the shelf life of the end product. It also enhances the flavors of many ingredients, including fruit and chocolate. Salt comes in several forms, including fine, coarse, sea, Himalayan, and kosher.

Spices. Spices have a way of making your house smell like memories. Cinnamon, nutmeg, and ginger, for example, are often associated with the winter holidays. Spices can lose potency over time, so buy them in small amounts. For the best results, grind whole spices in a coffee grinder reserved for that purpose to make freshly ground versions right before baking.

CHOCOLATE AND COCOA

Aaaah, chocolate. You bring so much joy to so many. However, people with food allergies and sensitivities to milk must be hypervigilant about how their chocolate is processed. If you need to stay away from even microscopic amounts of dairy products, avoid chocolate that includes this statement on the label: "may contain traces of milk." This statement means that the chocolate was made in a factory or on equipment that was also used for milk chocolate, even if the chocolate itself is dairy-free.

Note that even nondairy chocolate may include soy derivatives or barley malt, which is a syrupy sweetener that contains gluten. But never fear. Even those who have dairy and gluten sensitivities can choose from a number of safe chocolate sources. One particularly good bet is semisweet chocolate chips (but, as always, read labels and call manufacturers when in doubt).

Chocolate Chips and Chunks

Nondairy semisweet chocolate chips and chunks are available from allergen-free sources, and thankfully, they're delicious and work wonderfully in baking and desserts. Enjoy Life brand makes nondairy semisweet mini chocolate chips and chunks and guarantees their allergen-free status. Other forms of chocolate, such as dark, white, or milk, aren't included in this book, primarily because they contain or have a high probability of being cross-contaminated with gluten, dairy products, or other allergens.

Melting Chocolate Chips

A number of recipes in this book call for melted nondairy semisweet chocolate chips. Two easy ways to melt chocolate chips are in a microwave or on the stove top using a double boiler. To melt chocolate chips in the microwave, put them in a microwave-safe bowl. Microwave on high for 15 seconds and stir. Repeat until the chocolate has melted and is smooth.

To melt chocolate on the stove top, put about 1 inch of water in a small saucepan. Bring to a simmer over medium heat. Put a glass bowl on top of the saucepan, making sure it doesn't touch the water but creates a seal with the saucepan to trap the steam produced by the simmering water. Put the chocolate chips in the bowl. As the bowl heats, the chocolate will melt. Stir occasionally, until the chocolate is completely melted. Use as directed.

Cacao and Cocoa

Cacao beans are the dried seeds of the cacao tree and are used to make chocolate and cocoa. Many types of cocoa, especially cocoa powders, work great for all kinds of baking. Following are the various types of cacao and unsweetened cocoa products used in the recipes in this book.

Cacao butter. Also known as cocoa butter, this highly aromatic ingredient is the pure fat extracted from the cacao bean. It's essential for making homemade white chocolate (see page 73).

Cacao nibs. Available sweetened or unsweetened, cacao nibs are made from roasted cacao beans. The nibs are crunchy and bitter, with a flavor similar to unsweetened cocoa powder.

Dutch-processed cocoa powder. Dutch-processed cocoa powder is treated with an alkali to neutralize cocoa's natural acidity. It's milder than natural cocoa powder and has a rich but delicate flavor.

Natural unsweetened cocoa powder. Natural cocoa powder is very bitter and has a deep chocolate flavor. It reacts with baking soda to create leavening action.

Unsweetened dark cocoa powder. Dark cocoa powder adds a very rich, dark-chocolate taste. It's typically a blend of natural and Dutch-processed cocoa powders.

Interchanging Dutch-Processed and Natural Cocoa

It's easy to substitute one kind of cocoa for the other.

- For every 3 tablespoons of Dutch-processed cocoa powder called for in a recipe, use 3 tablespoons of natural cocoa powder plus ⅛ teaspoon of baking soda.
- For every 3 tablespoons of natural unsweetened cocoa powder called for in a recipe, use 3 tablespoons of Dutch-processed cocoa powder plus ⅛ teaspoon of cider vinegar or lemon juice.

EGG-FREE, DAIRY-FREE, AND ALLERGY-FREE

Because my diet is vegan, I avoid the use of eggs and dairy products in my recipes. And even if you're not vegan, here's the deal: not only will you be cutting out common allergens (and making the recipes accessible to others), but you'll also be using substitutions that can provide an even better outcome.

Instead of Eggs

Though eggs aren't used often in pastry, custard-based recipes, such as puddings or ice creams, typically rely on eggs as an ingredient. It's easy to find a replacement, though. You can select the appropriate substitute simply by knowing the egg's task in a given recipe. Table 3 (page 22) provides all the details you need for replacing eggs in your own recipes.

Other common egg replacements are soy-based (silken tofu), leave an aftertaste (mashed legumes or beans), or require an extra purchase (premixed commercial egg replacer). For those reasons, I recommend the options outlined in table 3.

TABLE 3 Common egg substitutes and their uses

SUBSTITUTE FOR 1 EGG*	BEST USED IN	PURPOSE	NOTES
3 tablespoons warm water whisked with 1 tablespoon ground flaxseeds or chia seeds; let stand until thickened	Breads, cakes, cookies, muffins, scones	Binder	• Adds fiber and good fats • Too much can create a gummy texture • Use golden flaxseeds to avoid brown specks in light-colored baked goods
¼ cup mashed or puréed fruit (such as applesauce, avocado, banana, or pumpkin) plus ¼ teaspoon baking powder	Breads, cakes, cupcakes, muffins	Moisturizer	• Adds moisture and density • For 2 eggs, use ½ cup fruit plus only ¼ teaspoon baking powder
2 to 3 tablespoons nut or seed butter	Bars, brownies, muffins	Binder	• Adds density and flavor
1 to 3 tablespoons arrowroot starch or tapioca flour	Puddings, sauces, toppings	Thickener	• Start with 1 tablespoon and add more until the desired thickness is achieved
3 to 4 tablespoons nondairy milk plus ¼ teaspoon baking powder	Breads, cakes, cupcakes, muffins	Moisturizer	• Adds moisture • For 2 eggs, use 6 to 8 tablespoons nondairy milk plus only ¼ teaspoon baking powder

*If you're looking for an egg substitution for a conventional recipe, keep in mind that two egg whites is the equivalent of one egg.

Instead of Milk

Moo-ve over milk! Of the many nondairy milks you can choose from, unsweetened almond milk and coconut milk beverage work best for baking: they're thick, creamy, and don't add extra sweetness to the recipe. Here are the details on the most popular varieties of nondairy milk and when to use each one.

Almond milk. Because of its naturally sweet and nutty flavor, almond milk is an ideal ingredient for desserts. With a higher fat content than other nondairy milks, almond milk is thick and rich, making it an excellent baking staple.

Coconut milk beverage. Coconut milk beverage is sold in cartons and designed for drinking, and it works similarly to almond milk. It is not, however, the same as canned coconut milk.

Coconut milk (canned). Both lite and full-fat varieties of canned coconut milk have a high fat content that adds tenderness to baked goods. Full-fat canned coconut milk is essential for making ice cream and replacing cream (page 119). When refrigerated, full-fat canned coconut milk separates so that a thick, rich coconut cream (see below) concentrates at the top of the can and a thinner liquid settles to the bottom. In some recipes (see Whipped Topping, page 24), just the coconut cream is used.

Coconut Cream

Full-fat canned coconut milk yields a luscious coconut cream that can replace heavy cream, half-and-half, or whipping cream. For the highest fat percentage (and the creamiest cream), refrigerate cans of coconut milk for at least 24 hours. Carefully open the can, without shaking or tipping it. Use a spoon to scrape out the hardened cream, which can be used in recipes or made into Whipped Topping (page 24).

Rice milk. Rice milk has a thin texture and lacks the fat that gives baking a boost. In addition, its natural sweetness can alter the taste of the recipe. For these reasons, I don't recommend rice milk for use in baking and don't include rice milk in the recipes in this book.

Soy milk. If you consume soy, soy milk works well in baking; however, baked goods made with soy milk tend to brown more quickly than those made with other nondairy milks. Soy milk isn't used in the recipes in this book.

Vegan Buttermilk

I use the term "vegan buttermilk" in my recipes to provide a nondairy alternative to the classic baking ingredient. To make vegan buttermilk, put 1 tablespoon of cider vinegar in a liquid measuring cup. Add as much unsweetened nondairy milk as necessary to equal the total amount of vegan buttermilk called for in the recipe. Stir and let stand for about 10 minutes, until the mixture is clumpy and curdled. Other than rice milk, all nondairy milks work well using this method.

Whipped Topping

Free of: nuts, peanuts, seeds, yeast *Yield: about 2½ cups*

When you're preparing Whipped Topping, remember to put the canned coconut milk in the refrigerator 24 hours before using so that it's fully chilled. Note that different brands of coconut milk yield different amounts of cream.

2 (14-ounce) cans full-fat coconut milk, refrigerated at least 24 hours
1 tablespoon confectioners' sugar, sifted
1 teaspoon vanilla extract

Put the bowl and beaters from a stand mixer, or a large metal bowl and the wire beaters from an electric hand mixer, in the freezer for 20 minutes. Remove the bowl and beaters from the freezer and the coconut milk cans from the refrigerator. Don't shake the cans. Carefully open each can and spoon out the hardened coconut cream from the top of each can. Put the coconut cream, confectioners' sugar, and vanilla extract in the metal bowl. Using a stand mixer or hand mixer fitted with the chilled wire beaters, beat on high speed until creamy and fluffy, about 5 minutes. Refrigerate until needed.

Per ¼ cup: 151 calories, 1 g protein, 15 g fat (12 g sat), 4 g carbohydrates, 20 mg sodium, 0 mg calcium, 0 g fiber

ESSENTIAL EQUIPMENT

We know what's needed for general baking success—mixing bowls, whisks and spatulas, dry and liquid measuring cups—but when it comes to pies and desserts, there are several more indispensable items to keep on hand.

Baking pans and dishes. Baking pans come in many shapes and sizes. Muffin pans are used for making single-serving tarts. Note that dark metal pans, including nonstick pans, produce a darker crust. In addition, desserts will bake more quickly in darker pans. Glass baking dishes are often used for cobblers and similar desserts.

Baking sheets. Also called cookie sheets, baking sheets are flat, metal pans used for baking cookies and galettes; they're also handy for catching drips under juicy pies. Desserts and treats bake more quickly on dark and nonstick baking sheets.

Bench scraper. Also called a pastry scraper or dough scraper, a bench scraper is a small metal rectangle that is used to cut and move dough on work surfaces.

Grater. Fine graters, such as those made by Microplane, are used to zest citrus and are also excellent for grating fresh ginger and nutmeg.

Parchment paper. Parchment paper is used to line baking sheets to create a nonstick surface. An alternative is a reusable silicone baking mat, such as Silpat brand. Low-end versions aren't recommended as they won't be as durable.

Pastry blender. A pastry blender is used to cut cold fat into dry ingredients when making pastry. It's also helpful for mashing avocados and bananas.

Pastry brush. A pastry brush is used for brushing glaze or nondairy milk on pastries. It typically has a wooden or plastic handle with natural or synthetic bristles, such as silicone.

Pastry mat. A pastry mat is a large, plastic mat with measurements indicated on it for rolling out and measuring dough. The mat provides a clean workspace, helps keep counters clean, and is easier to use than waxed or parchment paper.

Pastry wheel. A pastry wheel is used to cut and shape pastry. It consists of a handle mounted to an axle that holds a blade for cutting or crimping dough.

Pie plates. I recommend ceramic pie plates, which are excellent heat conductors, or tempered glass pie plates, which disperse heat well. In comparison, metal pie pans are poor heat conductors.

Pie weights. Pie weights are used when blind baking a crust (see page 31). They weigh down the dough so it doesn't puff or shrink while baking. You can use ceramic pie weights, dried beans, or uncooked rice.

Rolling pin. There are two kinds of rolling pins: roller-style pins, which have a thick roller with small handles on the ends, and rod (or French) rolling pins, which are thinner with tapered ends. Both are usually made from wood but may also be made from glass, marble, silicone, or stainless steel.

Sieve. A fine-mesh sieve can be used to sift cocoa powder and confectioners' sugar with ease.

Tart pan. Tart pans have short, fluted sides and removable bottoms. They're sold in many shapes and sizes; the recipes in this book use a standard 9½-inch tart pan.

Tart tamper. A tart tamper is a double-sided tool that can be used to form and flatten dough into muffin cups to make tart crusts. It also can be used to press crusts into pans without the dough getting warm from your fingertips.

SEVEN TIPS FOR SUCCESS

I'm sure by now you're raring to go and have bookmarked a few recipes (or more than a few!) that are calling your name. For the best results, take a look through these tips before getting started.

1. Read the recipe. Sounds obvious, right? But it's important to read the recipe several times before starting so you have an idea of the steps involved. Plus, you can have all the equipment and ingredients ready to go, so you'll be less likely to forget something.

2. Glance through the chapter opening. At the beginning of each chapter, there are specific tips for creating the perfect pies, cobblers, ice creams, and other desserts. So after you pick your recipe—a pie, for example—revisit the special instructions and tips at the beginning of the pie chapter.

3. Spoon and level. Use the spoon-and-level method for measuring flours. Stir the flour just before using to aerate it in its container. Then spoon the flour into the measuring cup and level it off with the smooth edge of a table knife.

4. Measure carefully. Accuracy is critical to success in baking, so take your time when measuring each ingredient.

5. Combine dry ingredients thoroughly. Always use a dry whisk to combine dry ingredients, such as flours, leaveners, starches, and spices, before mixing them with wet ingredients. This will ensure that the dry mixture is aerated and the ingredients are evenly distributed.

6. Preheat the oven even longer than you need to. Preheat the oven for at least 15 minutes to be sure the temperature is accurate. Although most ovens will signal that they are ready earlier, don't believe them.

7. Store it right. If you have leftovers, be sure to check the beginning of each chapter for how to store all your delicious desserts for next-day noshing!

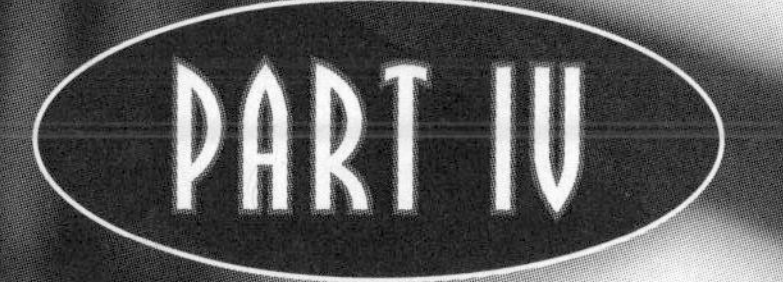

The Recipes

Pies & Cheesecakes

All you need is love. But a little chocolate now and then doesn't hurt.

CHARLES M. SCHULZ, AMERICAN CARTOONIST AND CREATOR OF PEANUTS

See Chocolate Mousse and Brownie Pie, page 50.

There's something undeniably special about a flaky crust loaded with fruit filling or chocolate mousse. The classic fruit pie is a perennial favorite, of course, and there are many variations in this chapter, from apple to berry to cherry to peach. Or try pies with fudgy brownie crusts or nut crusts and creamy fillings. Plus, satisfy the cheesecake lovers in your life with sweet, cheese-free versions (see below). I offer pies and cheesecakes to please everyone's palate; and to make them just that much more dreamy, don't forget to top them off with Whipped Topping (page 24) or a delicious dairy-free ice cream (page 118).

Cheesecakes without the Cheese

The three cheesecakes in this chapter—chocolate-cherry, coconut, and pumpkin—feature popular flavors but no actual cheese or even soy imitations. But trust me. In place of soy-based vegan cream cheese or tofu, I use coconut and nuts, which provide a rich texture while also offering many essential nutrients. I avoid soy-based products because soy is a common allergen, and soy isn't used in this book. For the best results, all you need is a good food processor, a little patience . . . and a love for cheesecake.

TIPS FOR PERFECT PIES

Pastry making—dare I say it—can be as easy as pie. Here are some key tips for producing a perfect pie, every time.

- For a flaky crust, the flours, fat, and water must be cold. If these ingredients aren't thoroughly chilled before mixing, the flours will absorb the fat, giving the crust a tough texture. Cold ingredients release moisture while they're baking, which results in a flaky and tender crust.
- Store flours in the refrigerator and make the water cold by putting it in the freezer for 20 minutes before using. When using vegan buttery spread, cut the buttery spread into ½-inch pieces and put the pieces in the freezer for 20 minutes before making the crust.
- Refrigerate kitchen gear, such as bowls, food-processor blades, and pastry blenders, for about 30 minutes before using.
- Roll out the pastry dough on waxed paper. This will make it easier to transfer the dough to the pie plate, which is important because gluten-free dough is more fragile than conventional dough.

- Roll out the pastry by positioning the rolling pin in the center of the dough and rolling outward; roll the dough in one direction only, not back and forth. This technique decreases sticking and tearing and ensures evenness.
- For the best results, consider investing in an Emile Henry pie plate, which bakes beautiful pies and is made of high-quality, ceramic-glazed stoneware.

PASTRY DOUGH THREE WAYS

Pastry dough can be made by hand, in a food processor, or with a stand mixer. Any of these three methods can be used to create a flaky, tender crust; however, for optimal texture, making the dough by hand is the way to go. Regardless of which method you choose, be sure to start with cold ingredients and don't overhandle the dough or it may become tough.

Hand Method

Put the flour and the other dry ingredients in a medium bowl and stir with a dry whisk until the ingredients are well combined. Using a pastry blender or two knives, cut the vegan buttery spread (or other fat; see sidebar, page 30) into the flour mixture until the texture resembles coarse crumbs; the pieces of buttery spread should be no larger than peas. Mix 2 tablespoons of the water with the cider vinegar and any other liquid ingredients called for in the recipe. Drizzle the liquid mixture over the flour mixture, a little at a time, mixing with a fork just until the dough starts to come together. Sprinkle with a bit of additional water if needed to make the dough come together. The mixture will seem drier than it should be; this will be remedied when you knead it. See "For All Methods," page 30.

Food-Processor Method

Fit the food processor with the metal S blade. Put the flour and other dry ingredients in the food processor and pulse about ten times until the ingredients are well combined. Add the vegan buttery spread (or other fat; see sidebar, page 30) and pulse six to eight times until the buttery spread breaks down into pea-sized clumps and is well distributed throughout the flour mixture. Mix 2 tablespoons of the water with the cider vinegar and any other liquid ingredients called for in the recipe. Drizzle about half the liquid mixture over the flour mixture. Pulse about five times, just until the dough starts to stick together, sprinkling with a bit of additional water if needed. The mixture will seem drier than it should be; this will be remedied when you knead it. See "For All Methods," below.

Stand-Mixer Method

Fit a stand mixer with the paddle attachment. Put the flour and other dry ingredients in the mixer bowl and stir with a dry whisk until the ingredients are well combined. Add the vegan buttery spread (or other fat; see sidebar, below) and mix on medium-low speed until the buttery spread breaks down into pea-sized clumps and is well distributed throughout the flour mixture. Mix 2 tablespoons of the water with the cider vinegar and any other liquid ingredients called for in the recipe. Drizzle about half the liquid mixture over the flour mixture. Mix on low speed just until the dough starts to stick together, sprinkling with a bit of additional water if needed. The mixture will seem drier than it should be; this will be remedied when you knead it. See "For All Methods," below.

For All Methods

Put a 12-inch square piece of waxed paper on a work surface and dust the waxed paper lightly with tapioca flour. Transfer the dough onto the waxed paper. Knead the dough two or three times until it fully comes together. The dough should not be dry or sticky. Form the dough into a disk. (If making a double crust, make two disks). Continue with the recipe as directed. Note that unlike conventional recipes, my recipes specify chilling the dough *after* it is rolled out.

To flute the crust, trim the dough after patting it into the pie plate, leaving about 1 inch hanging over the side of the pie plate. Fold the overhanging dough under itself to create an edge. Crimp the edge using your thumb and index finger, or use a fork, spoon, or crimping tool to create a decorative edge. For double crusts, fold the overhanging top and bottom crusts under, then crimp gently but firmly to ensure the crusts stay together during baking.

Making an Oil-Based Pastry Crust

Though vegan buttery spread makes the flakiest, best-tasting pastry, you can also use coconut oil if you prefer a different option. The substitution is simple: use 6 tablespoons of softened, not melted, coconut oil in place of the ½ cup of vegan buttery spread called for in the Buttery Pastry Crust (page 42), Cinnamon-Teff Pastry Crusts (page 74), or Teff Pastry Crust (pages 38). Then continue to prepare the recipe as directed.

SPECIAL TECHNIQUES

Parbaking and Blind Baking

I use parbaking and blind baking in some of my recipes. You may find these techniques helpful when experimenting with your own recipes.

Parbaking means partially baking a single pie crust before adding the filling, so the pie crust doesn't get soggy from a juicy or moist filling. Not all pies need to be parbaked. To parbake a crust, follow the instructions in the Pumpkin Pie with Pecan Streusel recipe (page 38).

Blind baking means using pie weights to weigh down an unfilled, single pie crust while baking so it doesn't puff up or shrink. You can use ceramic pie weights, dried beans, or uncooked rice. To blind bake a crust, follow the instructions in the Cranberry Pie with Maple Cashew Cream recipe (page 42).

Storing Pies, Tarts, and Cheesecakes

Most pies can be served about 4 hours after baking, while still a little warm. This amount of time is usually sufficient to allow the filling to set. In general, most crusts are flakiest the day they're made. Fruit pies and tarts, including tarts with cake-like filling, can be loosely covered and stored at room temperature for 2 days and refrigerated for an additional 2 days. (Some parts of the dessert, such as crisp crumble toppings, may soften.) Pies with creamy fillings and cheesecakes can be loosely covered and stored in the refrigerator for 3 days.

TABLE 4 Troubleshooting when making pies and tarts

Problem	Possible causes and solutions
The crust is tough, dense, and lacks flakiness.	• The ingredients and crust may not have been cold enough. Be sure to chill the flour, fat, and water before mixing the crust.
The crust becomes too dark around the edges.	• Wrap thin strips of aluminum foil loosely around the rim of the pie midway through baking. The foil will help deflect the heat. • Use a crust shield, a reusable baker's tool that "shields" the edges of the crust to prevent overbrowning.
The pie overflows.	• Make slits in the top crust before putting the pie in the oven; this will allow the steam to escape during baking. • Juicy fillings may overflow; for easy cleanup, bake the pie on a lined baking sheet.
The filling is too runny.	• Before baking, add an extra tablespoon of the thickener the recipe calls for. • After baking, let the pie cool completely before slicing.

This is the perfect pie to make at summer's end, when peaches are at the peak of ripeness. The combination of juicy peaches and buttery, flaky crust is just like Grandma used to make.

PEACH PIE WITH BUTTERY Double Crust

FREE OF: NUTS, PEANUTS, SEEDS

YIELD: 8 SLICES

PEACH FILLING

3½ pounds unpeeled peaches, sliced ¼ inch thick (about 10 peaches)

6 tablespoons unrefined cane sugar

3½ tablespoons tapioca flour

1 tablespoon freshly squeezed lemon juice

¼ teaspoon salt

⅛ teaspoon ground cinnamon

BUTTERY PASTRY CRUST *(Double)*

1½ cups sorghum flour

⅓ cup quinoa flour

⅓ cup arrowroot starch

⅓ cup tapioca flour, plus more for rolling

1 tablespoon unrefined cane sugar

1¼ teaspoons xanthan gum

½ teaspoon fine sea salt

1 cup vegan buttery spread, cut into ½-inch cubes and put in the freezer for 20 minutes

2 tablespoons ice water, plus more if needed

1 teaspoon cider vinegar

1 teaspoon vanilla extract

To make the filling, put half the peaches in a large bowl. Put the remaining peaches in a large saucepan and cook over medium-high heat until the peaches begin to break down and become juicy (very ripe peaches will require less time to cook). Put the sugar and tapioca flour in a small bowl and stir until well combined. Sprinkle the mixture over the peaches in the saucepan. Cook, stirring constantly, until thickened, about 2 minutes. Stir in the lemon juice, salt, and cinnamon. Add the cooked mixture to the peaches in the bowl and stir until well combined. Let cool to room temperature.

To make the crust, put a 12-inch square piece of waxed paper on a work surface. Lightly coat a 9-inch deep-dish glass pie plate with vegan buttery spread.

Put the sorghum flour, quinoa flour, arrowroot starch, tapioca flour, sugar, xanthan gum, and salt in a medium bowl, food processor, or the bowl of a stand mixer and stir with a dry whisk to combine. Follow one of the methods on page 29 for making the dough, adding the buttery spread, water, vinegar, and vanilla extract and dividing the dough into disks as directed.

Wrap one of the disks of dough in plastic wrap and put it in the refrigerator. Put the second disk in the middle of the waxed paper. Lightly dust a rolling pin with tapioca flour and roll out the dough, forming a circle about 12 inches in diameter and ⅛ inch thick. (The dough should roll easily; if it's too dry, sprinkle it with up to 1 tablespoon of additional water and knead the water into the dough.) Use the waxed paper to carefully invert the dough onto the prepared pie plate. Leaving the waxed paper on, ease the dough into the pie plate, using your fingers to pat the dough into the bottom and up

Per slice: 471 calories, 6 g protein, 24 g fat (6 g sat), 63 g carbohydrates, 415 mg sodium, 14 mg calcium, 6 g fiber

the sides of the pie plate to form the bottom crust. Carefully peel off the waxed paper and trim the dough with a butter knife, leaving a 1-inch overhang. Put the bottom crust in the freezer for 30 minutes.

Dust the waxed paper with more tapioca flour. Remove the remaining disk of dough from the refrigerator and put it on the waxed paper. This will be the top crust. Roll out the dough, forming a circle about 12 inches in diameter and ⅛ inch thick. Leaving the waxed paper on, put the top crust on a cutting board or other flat surface and refrigerate.

To fill and bake the pie, position one oven rack on the lowest level and a second oven rack in the middle of the oven. Preheat the oven to 425 degrees F. Remove the bottom crust from the freezer and spoon the filling into it. Remove the top crust from the refrigerator. Leaving the waxed paper on, carefully invert the top crust onto the filling. Carefully peel off the waxed paper and trim the dough with a butter knife, leaving about a 1-inch overhang. Flute the edges to seal the crusts together (see page 30). Cut five slits in the top crust using a sharp knife (this will allow the steam to escape during baking). Put the pie in the freezer for 15 minutes.

Remove the pie from the freezer and put it on a baking sheet. Bake on the lowest rack for 15 minutes. Transfer the pie with the baking sheet to the middle rack. Decrease the oven temperature to 375 degrees F. Without waiting for the oven temperature to adjust, continue baking the pie for 50 to 55 minutes longer, until the crust is golden and the filling is bubbling. Let cool completely before serving.

When it comes to making cherry pie, sour cherries are superior to their sweeter counterparts, producing a sweet yet tart filling. Here, the cherries top a flaky crust studded with cacao nibs. In lieu of a traditional double crust, this recipe creates flair by using decorative cutouts for the top of the pie.

Cherry Pie WITH CACAO NIB PASTRY CRUST

FREE OF: NUTS, PEANUTS, SEEDS

YIELD: 8 SLICES

SOUR CHERRY FILLING

6 cups unsweetened fresh or thawed frozen pitted sour cherries, well drained, juice reserved

¾ cup unrefined cane sugar

¼ cup tapioca flour

CACAO NIB PASTRY CRUST

1¼ cups sorghum flour

¼ cup quinoa flour

¼ cup arrowroot starch

¼ cup tapioca flour, plus more for rolling

¼ cup unsweetened cacao nibs (see tip)

2 tablespoons unrefined cane sugar

1 teaspoon xanthan gum

¼ teaspoon fine sea salt

¾ cup vegan buttery spread, cut into ½-inch cubes and put in the freezer for 20 minutes

3 tablespoons ice water, plus more as needed

1 teaspoon vanilla extract

½ teaspoon cider vinegar

To make the filling, put the cherries in a medium saucepan. If using fresh cherries, cook over medium-high heat until the cherries begin to break down and are juicy. If using thawed frozen cherries, which will already be broken down, cook just until the cherries are juicy. Fresh and frozen cherries will yield different amounts of juice; cook until there's ½ to ⅔ cup of juice in the saucepan. If the frozen cherries don't produce that much juice, add the juice reserved from draining them. Bring the cherries to a boil. Put the sugar and tapioca flour in a small bowl and stir until well combined. Sprinkle the mixture over the cherries. Cook, stirring constantly, until thickened, about 2 minutes. Let cool to room temperature.

To make the crust, put a 12-inch square piece of waxed paper on a work surface. Lightly coat a 9-inch deep-dish glass pie plate with vegan buttery spread.

Put the sorghum flour, quinoa flour, arrowroot starch, tapioca flour, cacao nibs, sugar, xanthan gum, and salt in a medium bowl, a food processor, or the bowl of a stand mixer and stir with a dry whisk to combine. Follow one of the methods on page 29 for making the dough, adding the buttery spread, water, vanilla extract, and vinegar as directed. Use about two-thirds of the dough to form a large disk and the remaining one-third to form a small disk.

Wrap the small disk in plastic wrap and put it in the refrigerator. Put the large disk in the middle of the waxed paper. Lightly dust a rolling pin with tapioca flour and roll out the dough, forming a circle about 12 inches in diameter and ⅛ inch thick. (The dough should roll easily; if it's too dry, sprinkle it with additional water and knead the water into the dough.) Use

Per slice: 447 calories, 5 g protein, 20 g fat (6 g sat), 66 g carbohydrates, 246 mg sodium, 25 mg calcium, 6 g fiber

the waxed paper to carefully invert the dough onto the prepared pie plate. Leaving the waxed paper on, ease the dough into the pie plate, using your fingers to pat the dough into the bottom and up the sides of the pie plate to form the bottom crust. Carefully peel off the waxed paper and trim the dough with a butter knife, leaving a 1-inch overhang. Flute the crust (see page 30) and put it in the freezer for 30 minutes.

Dust the waxed paper with more tapioca flour. Remove the small disk of dough from the refrigerator and put it on the waxed paper. Roll out the dough until it is about 1/8 inch thick (it can be any shape). Using a knife, pastry blender, or cookie cutter, cut the dough into desired shapes. Keeping them on the waxed paper, transfer the cutouts to a cutting board or other flat surface. Refrigerate for 30 minutes, keeping the bottom crust in the freezer.

To fill and bake the pie, position an oven rack on the lowest level of the oven. Preheat the oven to 375 degrees F. Remove the crust from the freezer. Spoon the filling into the crust. Remove the cutouts from the refrigerator and arrange them, slightly overlapping, on top of the filling as desired. Put the pie in the freezer for 15 minutes.

Remove the pie from the freezer and put it on a baking sheet. Bake on the lowest rack for 50 to 60 minutes, until the crust is golden and the filling is bubbling. Let cool completely before serving.

TIP: Cacao nibs can vary in size; for this recipe, they should be small. Use a sharp knife to finely chop large nibs or clusters into small pieces before mixing them into the dry ingredients.

Loaded with raisins, this pie is also known as funeral pie, because it is traditionally served at a wake following a funeral—perhaps because the ingredients are readily available and the pie keeps well. Of course, that doesn't mean it isn't suitable as an anytime recipe! Brushing the crust with canned coconut milk adds extra flakiness, but any nondairy milk will do.

Old-Fashioned RAISIN PIE

FREE OF: NUTS, PEANUTS, SEEDS

YIELD: 10 SLICES

RAISIN FILLING

3½ heaping cups raisins

2½ cups water

⅓ cup unrefined cane sugar

3 tablespoons sorghum flour

3 tablespoons cider vinegar (see tip)

2 tablespoons tapioca flour

1½ teaspoons ground cinnamon

½ teaspoon fine sea salt

1 tablespoon vegan buttery spread

BUTTERY PASTRY CRUST *(Double)*

1½ cups sorghum flour

⅓ cup quinoa flour

⅓ cup arrowroot starch

⅓ cup tapioca flour, plus more for rolling

1 tablespoon unrefined cane sugar

1¼ teaspoons xanthan gum

½ teaspoon fine sea salt

1 cup vegan buttery spread, cut into ½-inch cubes and put in the freezer for 20 minutes

2 tablespoons ice water, plus more if needed

1 teaspoon cider vinegar

1 teaspoon vanilla extract

To make the filling, put the raisins, water, sugar, sorghum flour, vinegar, tapioca flour, cinnamon, and salt in a medium saucepan and whisk until well combined. Bring to a boil over medium-high heat. Cook, whisking frequently, until very thick, about 4 minutes. Remove from the heat, stir in the buttery spread, and let cool for 20 minutes.

To make the crust, put a 12-inch square piece of waxed paper on a work surface. Lightly coat a 9-inch deep-dish glass pie plate with vegan buttery spread.

Put the sorghum flour, quinoa flour, arrowroot starch, tapioca flour, sugar, xanthan gum, and salt in a medium bowl, a food processor, or the bowl of a stand mixer and stir with a dry whisk to combine. Follow one of the methods on page 29 for making the dough, adding the buttery spread, water, vinegar, and vanilla extract and dividing the dough into disks as directed.

Wrap one of the disks in plastic wrap and put it in the refrigerator. Put the second disk in the middle of the waxed paper. Lightly dust a rolling pin with tapioca flour and roll out the dough, forming a circle about 12 inches in diameter and ⅛ inch thick. (The dough should roll easily; if it's too dry, sprinkle it with up to 1 tablespoon of additional water and knead the water into the dough.) Use the waxed paper to carefully invert the dough onto the prepared pie plate. Leaving the waxed paper on, ease the dough into the pie plate, using your fingers to pat the dough into the bottom and up the sides of the pie plate to form a crust. Carefully peel off the waxed paper and trim the dough with a butter knife, leaving a 1-inch overhang. Put the crust in the freezer for 30 minutes.

Per slice: 508 calories, 5 g protein, 20 g fat (5 g sat), 83 g carbohydrates, 423 mg sodium, 32 mg calcium, 5 g fiber

FINISHING TOUCHES

1 tablespoon full-fat canned coconut milk or nondairy milk

Dust the waxed paper with more tapioca flour. Remove the remaining disk of dough from the refrigerator and put it on the waxed paper. This will be the top crust. Roll out the dough, forming a circle about 12 inches in diameter and ⅛ inch thick. Use a small cookie cutter to cut five shapes in the dough, both for decoration and to allow steam to escape, and reserve the cutouts. Leaving the waxed paper on, put the top crust on a cutting board or other flat surface and refrigerate.

To fill and bake the pie, position one oven rack on the lowest level and a second oven rack in the middle of the oven. Preheat the oven to 425 degrees F. Remove the bottom crust from the freezer and spoon the filling into it. Remove the top crust from the refrigerator. Leaving the waxed paper on, carefully invert the top crust onto the filling, leaving about a 1-inch overhang. Flute the edges to seal the crusts together (see page 30). Brush the pastry with the coconut milk. Decorate the crust with the cutouts, but don't cover the openings. Put the pie in the freezer for 15 minutes.

Remove the pie from the freezer and put it on a baking sheet. Bake on the lowest rack for 15 minutes. Transfer the pie with the baking sheet to the middle rack. Decrease the oven temperature to 375 degrees F. Without waiting for the oven temperature to adjust, continue baking the pie for 50 to 55 minutes longer, until the crust is golden and the filling is bubbling. Let cool completely before serving.

TIP: Cider vinegar is a traditional ingredient in raisin pie filling, but lemon juice is an appropriate substitute that adds a pleasing element. If you prefer a zing of lemon flavor, replace the vinegar with 3 tablespoons of freshly squeezed lemon juice.

In this rendition, classic pumpkin pie gets a flavorful makeover when it's topped with pecan streusel and nestled in a flaky teff pastry. If you prefer extra-spicy pumpkin pie, add more spices to the filling to taste.

PUMPKIN PIE WITH Pecan Streusel

FREE OF: PEANUTS, SEEDS

YIELD: 8 SLICES

TEFF PASTRY CRUST

¾ cup sorghum flour

¼ cup teff flour

¼ cup tapioca flour, plus more for rolling

1 tablespoon unrefined cane sugar

¾ teaspoon xanthan gum

¼ teaspoon fine sea salt

½ cup vegan buttery spread, cut into ½-inch cubes and put in the freezer for 20 minutes

2 tablespoons ice water, plus more as needed

1 teaspoon cider vinegar

PUMPKIN FILLING

2½ cups mashed cooked or canned pumpkin

½ cup unsweetened nondairy milk

⅓ cup pure maple syrup

⅓ cup unrefined cane sugar

3 tablespoons sorghum flour

3 tablespoons tapioca flour

2 teaspoons ground cinnamon

1 teaspoon vanilla extract

½ teaspoon ground ginger

½ teaspoon ground nutmeg

⅛ teaspoon ground cloves

⅛ teaspoon fine sea salt

To make the crust, put a 12-inch square piece of waxed paper on a work surface. Lightly coat a 9-inch glass pie plate with vegan buttery spread. Put the sorghum flour, teff flour, tapioca flour, sugar, xanthan gum, and salt in a medium bowl, a food processor, or the bowl of a stand mixer and stir with a dry whisk to combine. Follow one of the methods on page 29 for making the dough, adding the buttery spread, water, and vinegar as directed and forming a single disk.

Put the disk in the middle of the waxed paper. Lightly dust a rolling pin with tapioca flour and roll out the dough, forming a circle about 12 inches in diameter and ⅛ inch thick. (The dough should roll easily; if it's too dry, sprinkle it with additional water and knead the water into the dough.) Use the waxed paper to carefully invert the dough into the prepared pie plate. Leaving the waxed paper on, ease the dough into the pie plate, using your fingers to pat the dough into the bottom and up the sides of the pie plate to form a bottom crust. Carefully peel off the waxed paper and trim and flute the crust (see page 30). Prick the crust with a fork about twenty times. Put the crust in the freezer for 30 minutes.

To make the filling, put the pumpkin, nondairy milk, maple syrup, sugar, sorghum flour, tapioca flour, cinnamon, vanilla, ginger, nutmeg, cloves, and salt in a food processor. Process until well combined, stopping occasionally to scrape down the work bowl if necessary.

To make the topping, put the pecans, sugar, and sorghum flour in a small bowl and stir until well combined. Stir in the buttery spread until the pecans are coated and the mixture becomes moist crumbs. Refrigerate until needed.

Per slice: 360 calories, 4 g protein, 19 g fat (4 g sat), 47 g carbohydrates, 125 mg sodium, 70 mg calcium, 5 g fiber

PECAN STREUSEL TOPPING

¾ cup pecans, toasted (see sidebar, page 16), **cooled, and coarsely chopped**

3 tablespoons unrefined cane sugar

2 tablespoons sorghum flour

1½ tablespoons vegan buttery spread, softened

To parbake the crust, position an oven rack in the middle of the oven. Preheat the oven to 425 degrees F. Remove the crust from the freezer and gently press a sheet of aluminum foil or parchment paper into it. Fill with pie weights, dried beans, or uncooked rice. Bake on the middle rack for 20 minutes. Carefully remove the aluminum foil and weights and bake the crust for 5 to 10 minutes longer, until lightly golden. If the crust puffs up, gently press it down with a spatula.

To fill and bake the pie, remove the crust from the oven and spoon the filling into the crust. Decrease the oven temperature to 350 degrees F. Bake for 30 minutes.

Remove the pie from the oven. Sprinkle the topping over the filling, pressing it down lightly. Bake for 15 to 20 minutes longer, until the crust is golden and the edges of the filling are brown and dry to the touch. Let cool completely before serving.

Chocolate-Swirled Pumpkin Pie: Omit the streusel topping. Prepare the filling as directed, omitting the sugar. Set aside 1 cup of the pumpkin filling and spoon the remaining filling into the parbaked crust. Melt ⅔ cup of nondairy semisweet chocolate chips in a microwave or on the stove top (see page 20). Put the remaining cup of pumpkin filling in a small bowl and stir in the melted chocolate. Dollop the chocolate mixture on top of the pumpkin filling and swirl it in with a butter knife. Bake for 40 to 45 minutes, until the edges of the filling are brown and dry to the touch and the filling is dry.

Because I live near orchards, I have the opportunity to pick my own apples and then head home to bake a fresh apple pie. I like using Mutsu apples, which are grown nearby and have just the right balance of tart and sweet, but any baking apple will do (see page 17). In this deep-dish pie, the apples are subtly spiced, and the teff pastry crust adds an earthy element.

Deep-Dish APPLE CRUMB PIE

FREE OF: NUTS, PEANUTS, SEEDS

YIELD: 8 SLICES

TEFF PASTRY CRUST

- **¾ cup sorghum flour**
- **¼ cup teff flour**
- **¼ cup tapioca flour, plus more for rolling**
- **1 tablespoon unrefined cane sugar**
- **¾ teaspoon xanthan gum**
- **¼ teaspoon fine sea salt**
- **½ cup vegan buttery spread, cut into ½-inch cubes and put in the freezer for 20 minutes**
- **2 tablespoons ice water, plus more if needed**
- **1 teaspoon cider vinegar**

APPLE FILLING

- **5½ cups peeled and sliced apples** (see page 17), **about ⅛ inch thick** (about 6 apples)
- **⅓ cup unrefined cane sugar** (see tip)
- **3 tablespoons sorghum flour**
- **¾ teaspoon ground cinnamon**
- **¼ teaspoon ground cardamom**
- **¼ teaspoon fine sea salt**
- **⅛ teaspoon ground nutmeg**

CRUMB TOPPING

- **¾ cup sorghum flour**
- **½ cup unrefined cane sugar**
- **6 tablespoons vegan buttery spread**

To make the crust, put a 12-inch square piece of waxed paper on a work surface. Lightly coat a 9-inch glass pie plate with vegan buttery spread.

Put the sorghum flour, teff flour, tapioca flour, sugar, xanthan gum, and salt in a medium bowl, food processor, or the bowl of a stand mixer and stir with a dry whisk to combine. Follow one of the methods on page 29 for making the pastry, adding the buttery spread, water, and vinegar as directed and forming the dough into a single disk.

Put the disk in the middle of the waxed paper. Lightly dust a rolling pin with tapioca flour and roll out the dough, forming a circle about 12 inches in diameter and ⅛ inch thick. (The dough should roll easily; if it's too dry, sprinkle it with up to 1 tablespoon of additional water and knead the water into the dough.) Use the waxed paper to carefully invert the dough onto the prepared pie plate. Leaving the waxed paper on, ease the dough into the pie plate, using your fingers to pat the dough into the bottom and up the sides of the pie plate to form a crust. Carefully peel off the waxed paper and trim and flute the crust (see page 30). Prick the crust with a fork about twenty times. Put the crust in the freezer for 30 minutes.

To make the filling, put the apples, sugar, flour, cinnamon, cardamom, salt, and nutmeg in a large bowl. Stir until the apples are well coated.

To make the topping, put the sorghum flour and sugar in a small bowl and stir with a spoon until well combined. Use your fingers to rub in the buttery spread until the mixture forms small clumps.

To fill and bake the pie, position one oven rack on the lowest level and a second oven rack in the middle of the oven. Preheat

Per slice: 430 calories, 4 g protein, 20 g fat (5 g sat), 60 carbohydrates, 341 mg sodium, 12 mg calcium, 5 g fiber

the oven to 425 degrees F. Remove the crust from the freezer and spoon the filling into it.

Put the pie on a baking sheet. Loosely cover the pie with aluminum foil. Bake on the lowest rack for 15 minutes.

Remove the pie from the oven and carefully peel off the aluminum foil. Use your fingers to gently squeeze the topping over the apples, forming small clumps, until the apples are evenly covered. Transfer the pie with the baking sheet to the middle rack. Decrease the oven temperature to 375 degrees F. Without waiting for the oven temperature to adjust, continue baking for 30 minutes, then tent with aluminum foil to prevent the topping from burning. Bake for 55 to 70 minutes longer, until the crust is golden and the filling is bubbling. Let cool completely before serving.

TIP: Adjust the amount of sugar in the filling based on the type of apples you're using and your own preferences. If the apples are tart or you prefer a sweeter pie, use ½ cup of sugar. If the apples are very sweet or you prefer a tarter pie, ⅓ cup of sugar will do the trick.

Fall is the perfect time to make pies and tarts. After all, apples, pears, and pumpkin are plentiful, and cranberries also get a chance to shine. Lucky for you, they take the spotlight in this simple, autumn-inspired pie. If desired, swap the Maple Cashew Cream for Maple Ice Cream (page 123) and serve with a steaming mug of apple cider.

CRANBERRY PIE WITH Maple Cashew Cream

FREE OF: PEANUTS, SEEDS

YIELD: 8 SLICES

BUTTERY PASTRY CRUST *(Single)*

- **¾ cup sorghum flour**
- **¼ cup quinoa flour**
- **¼ cup tapioca flour, plus more for rolling**
- **1 tablespoon unrefined cane sugar**
- **¾ teaspoon xanthan gum**
- **¼ teaspoon fine sea salt**
- **½ cup vegan buttery spread, cut into ½-inch cubes and put in the freezer for 20 minutes**
- **2 tablespoons ice water, plus more as needed**
- **2 teaspoons cider vinegar**

CRANBERRY FILLING

- **4 cups fresh or frozen cranberries**
- **½ cup pure maple syrup**
- **2 tablespoons finely grated orange zest**
- **1 tart apple** (see page 17), **peeled and grated**
- **3 tablespoons freshly squeezed orange juice**
- **2 tablespoons tapioca flour**

To make the crust, put a 12-inch square piece of waxed paper on a work surface. Lightly coat a 9-inch glass pie plate with vegan buttery spread.

Put the sorghum flour, quinoa flour, tapioca flour, sugar, xanthan gum, and salt in a medium bowl, a food processor, or the bowl of a stand mixer and stir with a dry whisk to combine. Follow one of the methods on page 29 for making the dough, adding the buttery spread, water, and vinegar as directed and forming a single disk.

Put the disk in the middle of the waxed paper. Lightly dust a rolling pin with tapioca flour and roll out the dough, forming a circle about 12 inches in diameter and ⅛ inch thick. (The dough should roll easily; if it's too dry, sprinkle it with additional water and knead the water into the dough.) Use the waxed paper to carefully invert the dough onto the prepared pie plate. Leaving the waxed paper on, ease the dough into the pie plate, using your fingers to pat the dough into the bottom and up the sides of the pie plate to form a crust. Carefully peel off the waxed paper and trim and flute the crust (see page 30). Prick the crust with a fork about twenty times. Put the crust in the freezer for 30 minutes.

Position an oven rack in the lower third of the oven. Preheat the oven to 425 degrees F. Remove the crust from the freezer and gently press a sheet of aluminum foil or parchment paper into it. Fill the crust with pie weights, dried beans, or uncooked rice.

Per slice: 368 calories, 5 g protein, 18 g fat (4 g sat), 47 g carbohydrates, 193 mg sodium, 43 mg calcium, 5 g fiber

MAPLE CASHEW CREAM *(can be prepared up to 2 days in advance)*

1 cup raw cashews, soaked for at least 4 hours, then drained

6 tablespoons unsweetened nondairy milk, plus more as desired

1½ tablespoons pure maple syrup

¼ teaspoon maple extract

¼ teaspoon vanilla extract

Pinch fine sea salt

Bake in the lower third of the oven for 20 minutes. Carefully remove the weights and aluminum foil. If the crust puffs up, gently press it down with a spatula. Decrease the oven temperature to 375 degrees F. Without waiting for the oven temperature to adjust, continue baking the crust for 15 to 20 minutes longer, until golden brown. Let cool completely before filling.

To make the filling, put the cranberries, maple syrup, orange zest, and apple in a medium saucepan and bring to a boil over medium heat. Cook, stirring occasionally, until the cranberries begin to pop, about 7 minutes. Put the orange juice and tapioca flour in a small bowl and whisk until smooth. Stir the orange juice mixture into the cranberry mixture. Decrease the heat to low and cook, stirring occasionally, for 10 to 15 minutes, until the apple is soft and the mixture is very thick. Let cool for 10 minutes.

To fill the pie, spoon the filling into the crust. Let cool completely.

To make the cashew cream, put the cashews, nondairy milk, maple syrup, maple extract, vanilla extract, and salt in a food processor. Process until completely smooth, adding additional nondairy milk until the preferred thickness is achieved. Put a dollop on top of each slice of pie just before serving, or pass the cashew cream at the table. Store leftover cashew cream in a sealed container in the refrigerator for up to 3 days.

This pie can be put together quickly and easily but should only be made when strawberries are at their ultimate ripeness—out-of-season strawberries just won't do. This recipe features a nut crust, but if you're craving a pastry crust instead, use the Buttery Pastry Crust (page 42) or the the oil-based crust (page 30), following the baking instructions for Cranberry Pie (page 42).

Fresh Strawberry Pie WITH ALMOND CRUST

FREE OF: CORN, PEANUTS, SEEDS, YEAST

YIELD: 8 SLICES

ALMOND CRUST

2 cups almonds

3 tablespoons agave nectar

4 teaspoons melted coconut oil

¼ teaspoon fine sea salt

STRAWBERRY FILLING

6 cups sliced strawberries, about ½ inch thick

⅓ cup unrefined cane sugar (see tip)

½ cup water

3 tablespoons tapioca flour

To make the crust, position an oven rack in the middle of the oven. Preheat the oven to 350 degrees F. Lightly oil a 9-inch glass pie plate.

Put the almonds in a food processor and process until finely ground. Transfer to a medium bowl. Stir in the agave nectar, coconut oil, and salt until well combined. Press the mixture evenly into the bottom and up the sides of the prepared pie plate to form a crust. Bake on the middle rack for 18 to 20 minutes, until firm. Let cool completely before filling.

To make the filling, put 1 heaping cup of the strawberries in the food processor and process until smooth. Scrape into a medium saucepan using a rubber spatula. Stir in the sugar and water until combined. Sprinkle the tapioca flour over the mixture and whisk until well combined. Cook over medium heat, whisking constantly, until the mixture begins to boil and thicken. Boil for 1 minute, then remove from the heat. Let cool for 10 minutes. Put the remaining strawberries in a medium bowl and pour the hot mixture over the strawberries, stirring gently to coat them.

To fill the pie, spoon the filling into the crust. Refrigerate for 4 hours before serving.

TIPS

- Increase the sugar to ½ cup if the strawberries aren't very sweet.
- Pie fillings that are thickened with tapioca flour can be a bit gooey at first but become firmer the longer the pie sits.

Per slice: 282 calories, 6 g protein, 17g fat (3 g sat), 63 g carbohydrates, 75 mg sodium, 100 mg calcium, 5 g fiber

The mousse-like lime filling is rich, silky, and both sweet and tart at the same time. It provides the perfect complement to the melt-in-your-mouth macadamia crust. Be sure to zest the limes before juicing them; you'll need about five limes to get the right amount of zest and juice.

CREAMY LIME PIE WITH Macadamia Crust

FREE OF: PEANUTS, SEEDS, YEAST

YIELD: 8 SLICES

MACADAMIA CRUST

1 cup dry-roasted salted macadamia nuts

¾ cup sorghum flour

3 tablespoons unrefined cane sugar

3 tablespoons vegan buttery spread, chilled

2 teaspoons unsweetened nondairy milk

LIME FILLING *(start preparation 24 hours in advance)*

1 (14-ounce) **can full-fat coconut milk, refrigerated at least 24 hours**

1½ cups mashed avocado flesh (about 2 large avocados)

2 tablespoons finely grated lime zest, packed (about 5 limes)

½ cup freshly squeezed lime juice

6 tablespoons agave nectar

1 teaspoon vanilla extract

¼ teaspoon fine sea salt

2 tablespoons coconut oil, melted

To make the crust, position an oven rack in the middle of the oven. Lightly oil a 9-inch glass pie plate. Preheat the oven to 350 degrees F.

Put the macadamia nuts, sorghum flour, and sugar in a food processor and process until the macadamia nuts are finely ground. Add the buttery spread and nondairy milk and pulse until the mixture sticks together in moist clumps. Press the mixture into the bottom and up the sides of the prepared pie plate to form a crust. Prick the crust with a fork about twenty times. Bake on the middle rack for 13 to 18 minutes, until firm and golden brown. Let cool completely before filling.

To make the filling, carefully open the can of coconut milk and spoon out the hardened coconut cream. Put the coconut cream, avocado flesh, lime zest, lime juice, agave nectar, vanilla extract, and salt in the food processor. Process until smooth and fluffy, about 3 minutes, stopping occasionally to scrape down the work bowl if necessary. With the food processor running, add the coconut oil in a thin stream and process for 1 minute.

To fill the pie, scrape the filling into the cooled crust using a rubber spatula. Refrigerate for 8 hours before serving. Serve chilled.

Per slice: 453 calories, 5 g protein, 35 g fat (15 g sat), 34 g carbohydrates, 172 mg sodium, 18 mg calcium, 5 g fiber

If you love peanut butter and chocolate, you'll love this pie—and we can be fast friends too. The bittersweet cocoa pastry crust holds a cake-like peanut butter filling that's studded with chocolate chips. You're just a few steps away from pure peanut butter bliss.

Peanut Butter BLONDIE PIE WITH COCOA CRUST

FREE OF: NUTS

YIELD: 10 SLICES

COCOA PASTRY CRUST

½ cup sorghum flour

¼ cup teff flour

¼ cup tapioca flour, plus more for rolling

¼ cup natural unsweetened cocoa powder, sifted

2 tablespoons unrefined cane sugar

¾ teaspoon xanthan gum

¼ teaspoon fine sea salt

½ cup vegan buttery spread, cut into ½-inch cubes and put in the freezer for 20 minutes

2 tablespoons ice water, plus more if needed

½ teaspoon cider vinegar

To make the crust, put a 12-inch square piece of waxed paper on a work surface. Lightly coat a 9-inch deep-dish glass pie plate with vegan buttery spread.

Put the sorghum flour, teff flour, tapioca flour, cocoa powder, sugar, xanthan gum, and salt in a medium bowl, a food processor, or the bowl of a stand mixer and stir with a dry whisk to combine. Follow one of the methods on page 29 for making the dough, adding the buttery spread, water, and vinegar as directed and forming the dough into a single disk. Wrap it in plastic wrap and put it in the refrigerator for 20 minutes.

Remove the dough from the refrigerator and put the disk in the middle of the waxed paper. Lightly dust a rolling pin with tapioca flour and roll out the dough, forming a circle about 12 inches in diameter and ⅛ inch thick. (The dough should roll easily; if it's crumbly or dry, sprinkle it with up to 1 tablespoon of additional water and knead the water into the dough.) Use the waxed paper to carefully invert the dough onto the prepared pie plate. Ease the dough into the prepared pie plate, using your fingers to pat the dough into the bottom and up the sides of the pie plate to form a crust. Carefully peel off the waxed paper and trim and flute the crust (see page 30). Refrigerate for 30 minutes.

To make the filling, put the water and flaxseeds in a small bowl and stir. Let stand until thickened, about 5 minutes. Put the sorghum flour, tapioca flour, and salt in a small bowl. Stir with a dry whisk to combine. Put the sugar, peanut butter, buttery spread, vanilla extract, and flaxseed mixture in the bowl of a stand mixer or a large bowl. Using the stand mixer or a hand mixer, beat on medium-high speed until well com-

Per slice: 470 calories, 7 g protein, 29 g fat (9 g sat), 51 g carbohydrates, 238 mg sodium, 10 mg calcium, 5 g fiber

PEANUT BUTTER BLONDIE FILLING

6 tablespoons warm water

2 tablespoons ground flaxseeds

6 tablespoons sorghum flour

2 tablespoons tapioca flour

⅛ teaspoon fine sea salt

¾ cup unrefined cane sugar

½ cup natural creamy peanut butter

¼ cup vegan buttery spread

1 teaspoon vanilla extract

1 cup nondairy semisweet chocolate chunks or chips

bined, about 2 minutes. Turn the mixer to low speed. Gradually add the flour mixture to the peanut butter mixture, beating until just combined to make a thick filling. Turn off the mixer. Stir in the chocolate chunks with a rubber spatula or wooden spoon.

To fill and bake the pie, position an oven rack in the lower third of the oven. Preheat the oven to 325 degrees F.

Scrape the filling evenly into the crust using a rubber spatula, smoothing the top. Bake for 50 to 60 minutes, until a knife inserted halfway between edge and center of the pie comes out clean. Let cool to room temperature before serving.

This dense, rich, and creamy pie is the stuff that dreams are made of, especially with the classic combination of hazelnuts and chocolate. The cookie crumbs for the crust are made from scratch, and the cocoa-dusted topping adds a final, elegant touch.

CHOCOLATE-HAZELNUT Truffle Pie

FREE OF: PEANUTS, SEEDS, YEAST

YIELD: 10 SLICES

COCOA COOKIE-CRUMB CRUST
(can be prepared up to 1 day in advance)

½ cup sorghum flour

½ cup natural unsweetened cocoa powder

⅓ cup unrefined cane sugar

1 tablespoon tapioca flour

½ teaspoon fine sea salt

¼ cup plus 1 tablespoon vegan buttery spread, melted

CHOCOLATE-HAZELNUT FILLING

1⅔ cups nondairy semisweet chocolate chips

1 cup roasted hazelnut butter (see sidebar, page 16)

½ cup unsweetened nondairy milk

2 tablespoons agave nectar

1 teaspoon vanilla extract

⅛ teaspoon fine sea salt

To make the crust, position an oven rack in the middle of the oven. Preheat the oven to 300 degrees F. Line a baking sheet with parchment paper or a Silpat liner. Lightly oil a 9-inch glass pie plate.

Put the sorghum flour, cocoa powder, sugar, tapioca flour, and salt in the bowl of a stand mixer or a large bowl and stir with a dry whisk to combine. Add ¼ cup of the buttery spread. Turn the stand mixer or a hand mixer on medium-low speed and beat until the mixture starts to come together in small clusters. Spread the mixture on the prepared baking sheet as thinly as possible. Bake on the middle rack for 20 minutes. Let cool completely. Increase the oven temperature to 350 degrees F.

Once the mixture has cooled, put it into a bowl and use your fingers to break it into crumbs. Add the remaining tablespoon of buttery spread and stir until well combined. Press the mixture firmly into the prepared pie plate, using your fingers to pat it into the bottom and partially up the sides of the pie plate to form a crust. The crust won't cover the sides completely. (If you find it difficult to press the mixture into the dish, simply spread it in the dish and put it in the freezer for 5 minutes. Then press it again—it will be easier to handle.) Put the crust in the freezer.

To make the filling, melt the chocolate chips using the microwave or stove-top method (see page 20). Put the hazelnut butter, nondairy milk, agave nectar, vanilla extract, and salt in a food processor and process until smooth. Add the melted chocolate and process until well combined.

To fill the pie, remove the crust from the freezer and scrape the filling into the crust using a rubber spatula. Refrigerate the pie.

Per slice: 563 calories, 10 g protein, 39 g fat (12 g sat), 50 g carbohydrates, 215 mg sodium, 131 mg calcium, 7 g fiber

HAZELNUT TOPPING

¾ cup hazelnuts, toasted (see sidebar, page 16)

1 tablespoon agave nectar

⅛ teaspoon fine sea salt

2 tablespoons natural unsweetened cocoa powder

To make the topping, put the hazelnuts, agave nectar, and salt in a small bowl and stir until well combined. Spread the hazelnuts on the prepared baking sheet and bake on the middle rack for 5 minutes, then stir and bake for 5 minutes longer. Return the hazelnuts to the bowl and stir in the cocoa powder until the hazelnuts are coated. Let cool.

Once the hazelnuts are cool, remove the pie from the refrigerator. Press the hazelnuts lightly into the filling so they stick. Refrigerate until the pie is completely firm before serving, about 3 hours.

Chocolate-Almond Truffle Pie: Use roasted creamy almond butter instead of the hazelnut butter, and almonds instead of the hazelnuts. See sidebar, page 16, for instructions for making homemade nut butters.

Chocolate lovers, get out your aprons! This dessert features a brownie that is baked in a pie plate, hollowed out to make a crust, loaded with a mousse filling made from an unexpected ingredient, then topped with brownie chunks and a sweet ganache. Chocolate nirvana.

Chocolate Mousse AND BROWNIE PIE

FREE OF: PEANUTS, YEAST

YIELD: 10 SLICES

CHOCOLATE MOUSSE FILLING
(prepare at least 1 day in advance)

2 cups mashed avocado flesh (about 4 avocados)

1 cup natural unsweetened cocoa powder

¾ cup agave nectar

1 tablespoon vanilla extract

¼ teaspoon fine sea salt

BROWNIE CRUST AND TOPPING

6 tablespoons brewed coffee

2 tablespoons ground flaxseeds

6 tablespoons vegan buttery spread

2 tablespoons roasted creamy cashew butter

1 cup unrefined cane sugar

½ cup sorghum flour

¼ cup tapioca flour

½ teaspoon baking powder

¼ teaspoon xanthan gum

½ cup plus 2 tablespoons natural unsweetened cocoa powder

2 teaspoons vanilla extract

⅛ teaspoon fine sea salt

To make the filling, put the avocado flesh, cocoa powder, agave nectar, vanilla extract, and salt in a food processor and process until smooth. Refrigerate for a minimum of 12 hours or up to 2 days.

To make the crust, position an oven rack in the middle of the oven. Preheat the oven to 325 degrees F. Lightly oil a 9-inch glass pie plate. Put the coffee and flaxseeds in the bowl of a stand mixer or a large bowl and stir to combine. Let stand until thickened, about 5 minutes.

Put the buttery spread and cashew butter in a small saucepan. Cook over medium heat, stirring occasionally, until melted. Stir in the sugar until well combined. Put the sorghum flour, tapioca flour, baking powder, and xanthan gum in a medium bowl. Stir with a dry whisk to combine.

Add the sugar mixture to the flaxseed mixture. Using the stand mixer or a hand mixer, beat on low speed until well combined. Turn off the mixer. Add the cocoa powder, vanilla extract, and salt and beat on medium speed until well combined. Turn the mixer to low speed. Slowly add the flour mixture, stopping occasionally to scrape down the bowl if necessary, and beat until well combined.

Scrape the filling evenly into the prepared pie plate using a rubber spatula, smoothing the top. Bake on the middle rack for about 25 minutes, until a toothpick inserted in the center comes out moist but with no gooey bits attached to it. Let cool completely.

Once the brownie has cooled, scoop out the center, leaving a ½-inch-thick rim around the edge and a thin layer of brownie on the bottom. To do this, score the brownie in a

Per slice: 415 calories, 5 g protein, 21 g fat (6 g sat), 60 g carbohydrates, 129 mg sodium, 32 mg calcium, 6 g fiber

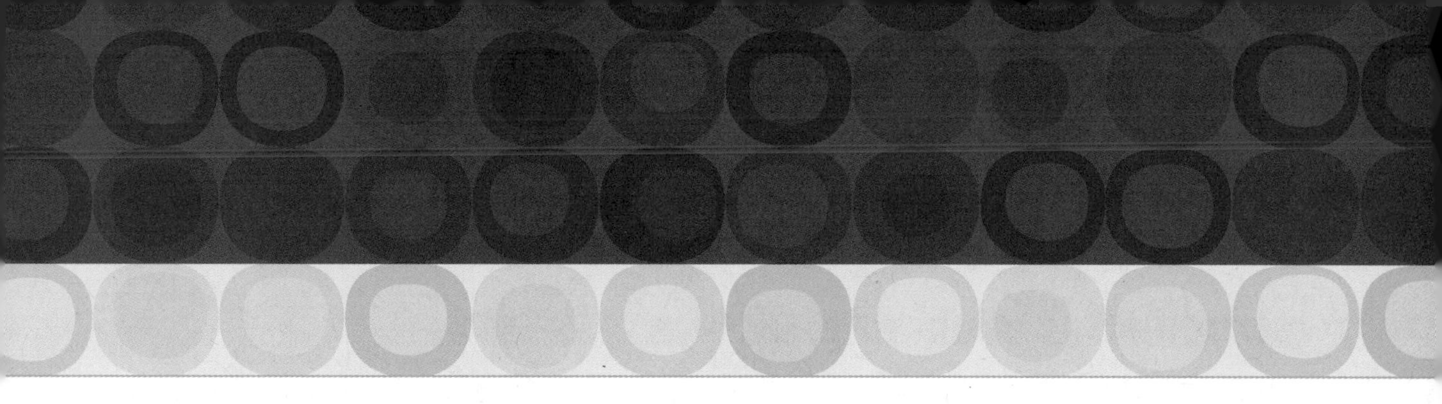

CHOCOLATE DRIZZLE

⅓ cup nondairy semisweet chocolate chips

1 tablespoon nondairy milk

crosshatch pattern using a sharp knife (leaving the ½-inch rim), then scoop out the pieces of brownie with a spoon, leaving the bottom layer to form a crust. The crust doesn't have to look perfect.

To fill the pie, spoon the filling into the crust. Top with the brownie pieces, pressing them down lightly.

To make the drizzle, melt the chocolate chips with the nondairy milk using the microwave or stove-top method (see page 20). Drizzle the mixture over the pie. Refrigerate for 2 hours before serving.

This creamy pie reminds me of the cheesecakes from my childhood—not like the dense New York–style cheesecakes, but lighter and silkier, like ones hailing from Philadelphia. Wild blueberries add the best flavor, but regular blueberries will work too.

Blueberries AND CREAM PIE

FREE OF: CORN, GRAINS, LEGUMES, PEANUTS, SEEDS, YEAST

YIELD: 8 SLICES

PECAN CRUST *(can be prepared up to 1 day in advance)*

- **2 cups pecans** (see tips)
- **½ cup pitted soft honey dates** (see page 14)

CREAMY BLUEBERRY FILLING

- **1 cup frozen wild blueberries, thawed but not drained**
- **1 ripe avocado, flesh mashed**
- **¾ cup creamy raw cashew butter** (see tips)
- **3 tablespoons agave nectar, plus more as needed**
- **2 tablespoons freshly squeezed lemon juice**
- **1 teaspoon vanilla extract**
- **⅛ teaspoon fine sea salt**
- **2 tablespoons coconut oil, melted**

BLUEBERRY TOPPING

- **1 cup frozen wild blueberries**
- **2 tablespoons agave nectar**

To make the crust, lightly oil a 9-inch glass pie plate. Put the pecans and dates in a food processor. Pulse until the ingredients begin to stick together. To test, squeeze a small amount of the mixture in your hand. If it doesn't stick together, pulse the mixture a few more times, being careful not to overprocess it.

Scrape the mixture into the prepared pie plate using a rubber spatula. Press the mixture evenly into the bottom and up the sides of the pie plate to form a crust. Put the crust in the freezer.

To make the filling, put the blueberries, avocado flesh, cashew butter, agave nectar, lemon juice, vanilla extract, and salt in the food processor. Process until smooth, stopping occasionally to scrape down the work bowl if necessary. Taste for sweetness—you may want to add 1 to 2 additional tablespoons of agave nectar if the blueberries aren't very ripe. The heat from the motor should slightly warm the mixture, which is good; otherwise, when you add the coconut oil, it will harden. With the food processor running, add the coconut oil in a thin stream and process until well combined.

To fill the pie, remove the crust from the freezer. Scrape the filling evenly into the crust using a rubber spatula, smoothing the top.

To make the topping, put the blueberries and agave nectar in the food processor and process until smooth. Spread the topping evenly over the filling using a rubber spatula, smoothing the top.

Put the pie back in the freezer if you're serving it within the hour, or put it in the refrigerator if you're serving it later in the day. Serve cold.

Per slice: 469 calories, 7 g protein, 36 g fat (7 g sat), 34 g carbohydrates, 1 mg sodium, 48 mg calcium, 6 g fiber

TIPS

- Toast the pecans (see page 16) if desired for a richer flavor, or leave them raw for a more subtle flavor.
- Either raw or roasted cashew butter works well in this recipe; the raw variety gives a more neutral flavor, while the roasted version adds depth and richness. To learn how to make homemade nut butter, see page 16.

Rich, thick, and creamy, this cheesecake is made with a graham-style crust and loaded with coconut flavor. The dried coconut and coconut milk form a luscious filling that's too good to pass up.

Coconut Cream CHEESECAKE

FREE OF: NUTS, PEANUTS, SEEDS, YEAST

YIELD: 12 SLICES

GRAHAM-STYLE COOKIE-CRUMB CRUST *(can be prepared up to 1 day in advance)*

¾ cup sorghum flour

½ cup teff flour

½ cup unrefined cane sugar

¼ cup tapioca flour

1 teaspoon xanthan gum

½ teaspoon fine sea salt

½ teaspoon ground cinnamon

½ cup vegan buttery spread, melted

6 tablespoons nondairy milk

2 tablespoons pure maple syrup

COCONUT CHEESECAKE FILLING

4 cups unsweetened finely shredded dried coconut

1 (14-ounce) **can full-fat coconut milk**

¼ cup raw or light agave nectar

½ teaspoon vanilla extract

¼ teaspoon fine sea salt

COCONUT TOPPING

¾ cup large flaked dried coconut, toasted (see sidebar, page 16)

To make the crust, position an oven rack in the middle of the oven. Preheat the oven to 300 degrees F. Line a baking sheet with parchment paper or a Silpat liner. Lightly oil a 9-inch glass pie plate.

Put the sorghum flour, teff flour, sugar, tapioca flour, xanthan gum, salt, and cinnamon in the bowl of a stand mixer or a large bowl. Stir with a dry whisk to combine. Add ¼ cup of the buttery spread and the nondairy milk. Turn the stand mixer or a hand mixer to low speed and mix until the mixture starts to come together in small clusters. Spread the mixture on the prepared baking sheet as thinly as possible. Bake on the middle rack for 20 to 22 minutes, until the mixture begins to feel firm to the touch. Let cool completely.

Once the mixture is cool, scrape it into a medium bowl using a rubber spatula, breaking up any large pieces until it's crumbly. Stir in the remaining ¼ cup of buttery spread and the maple syrup until well combined. The mixture should be sticky and hold together when squeezed in your hand. Press the mixture evenly into the bottom and up the sides of the prepared pie plate to form a crust. If the mixture is too sticky to work with, spread it in the pie plate and put it in the freezer for 5 minutes, then remove and press into a crust as directed. Put the crust in the freezer.

To make the filling, put the dried coconut in a food processor. Process on high speed until completely smooth, stopping occasionally to scrape down the work bowl if necessary. Processing can take up to 15 minutes, depending on the strength of the food processor. Keep a close eye on the coconut, which should turn into a smooth liquid. (If the coconut isn't processed

Per slice: 464 calories, 4 g protein, 33 g fat (25 g sat), 36 g carbohydrates, 237 mg sodium, 17 mg calcium, 6 g fiber

enough, the filling won't have the correct texture.) Add the coconut milk, agave nectar, vanilla extract, and salt to the coconut liquid and process for 5 minutes.

To fill the crust, remove the crust from the freezer. Spread the filling evenly in the crust using a rubber spatula, smoothing the top. Refrigerate for 30 minutes.

After the 30 minutes, the surface of the filling should be firm enough to support the topping, which should not sink into the filling. If the filling isn't firm enough, refrigerate the cheesecake for another 15 minutes. Sprinkle the topping over the filling, pressing it down lightly.

Refrigerate for 12 hours before serving. Serve cold.

TIP: If the coconut wasn't processed enough, the filling might not be very creamy. If that's the case, let the cheesecake stand at room temperature for about 20 minutes before serving. It will soften to a creamier texture.

DOUBLE CHOCOLATE-CHERRY Cheesecake

FREE OF: CORN, GRAINS, PEANUTS, SEEDS, YEAST

YIELD: 12 SLICES

BROWNIE-STYLE CRUST *(can be prepared up to 1 day in advance)*

1 cup almonds

¾ cup pecans

¾ cup pitted soft honey dates (see page 14)

3 tablespoons natural unsweetened cocoa powder

½ teaspoon fine sea salt

CHOCOLATE-CHERRY FILLING
(start preparation 24 hours in advance)

4 cups unsweetened finely shredded dried coconut

¼ cup coconut oil, melted

2¾ cups full-fat canned coconut milk, refrigerated at least 24 hours (see tip)

⅔ cup agave nectar

2 tablespoons freshly squeezed lemon juice

1 tablespoon vanilla extract

½ teaspoon fine sea salt

¾ cup natural unsweetened cocoa powder

1⅔ cups unsweetened pitted fresh or defrosted frozen sour cherries, well drained

To make the crust, lightly oil a 9-inch springform pan. If you don't have a springform pan, line a 9-inch round pan with aluminum foil; you can use the foil to easily remove the cheesecake from the pan once it has set.

Put the almonds, pecans, dates, cocoa powder, and salt in a food processor. Process until the ingredients begin to stick together, about 3 minutes. The almonds and pecans will be finely ground and the dates smooth. To test, squeeze a small amount of the mixture in your hand. If it doesn't stick together, pulse the mixture a few more times, being careful not to overprocess it. If it's not coming together, add 1 or 2 additional dates.

Scrape the mixture into the prepared pie plate using a rubber spatula, pressing it evenly on just the bottom of the pan with your fingers to form a crust. Put the crust in the freezer.

To make the filling, put the dried coconut and coconut oil in the food processor. Process on high speed until completely smooth, stopping occasionally to scrape down the work bowl if necessary. Processing can take up to 15 minutes, depending on the strength of the food processor. Keep a close eye on the coconut, which should turn into a smooth liquid. (If the coconut isn't processed enough, the filling won't have the correct texture.)

Pour the entire contents of one 14-ounce can (1¾ cups) of the coconut milk into the food processor. Carefully open the second can of coconut milk and spoon out the hardened coconut cream from the top of the can into a 1-cup measure. (Reserve the leftover coconut milk for another use.) Add the coconut cream to the food processor along with the agave nectar, lemon juice, vanilla extract, and salt. Process for 5 minutes.

Per slice: 530 calories, 7 g protein, 45 g fat (32 g sat), 28 g carbohydrates, 61 mg sodium, 48 mg calcium, 9 g fiber

DARK CHOCOLATE TOPPING

3 tablespoons natural unsweetened cocoa powder, preferably dark

3 tablespoons coconut oil, melted

1½ tablespoons agave nectar

1 teaspoon vanilla extract

⅛ teaspoon fine sea salt

The mixture may look like it's starting to separate and become fluffy, which is normal. Add the cocoa powder. Process until smooth and well combined, stopping occasionally to scrape down the work bowl if necessary.

To fill the crust, remove the crust from the freezer. Spread about half the filling evenly in the crust using a rubber spatula, smoothing the top. Put the crust in the freezer for 7 minutes. Spread the cherries evenly over the filling and the remaining filling on top of the cherries. Put the cheesecake in the freezer for 5 minutes.

To make the topping, put the cocoa powder, coconut oil, agave nectar, vanilla extract, and salt in a small bowl and stir until well combined. Remove the cheesecake from the freezer. Spread or drizzle the topping over the cheesecake.

Refrigerate, but don't freeze, the cheesecake for 12 hours before serving. To serve, remove the cheesecake from the pan and transfer it to a serving dish.

TIP: The coconut milk should be chilled in the can. You'll need to refrigerate two 14-ounce cans of coconut milk for 24 hours before making the cheesecake, but you'll only need one full can of the coconut milk and 1 cup of the coconut cream from the second can.

Raspberry-Chocolate Cheesecake: Replace the cherries in the filling with 1⅔ cups of fresh or thawed frozen raspberries, well drained.

Creamy, sweet pumpkin filling in a spicy ginger crust . . . you can't go wrong with this fall-inspired combination in a unique cheesecake. This no-bake dessert is easy to prepare in advance, making it the ideal addition to your holiday repertoire.

Pumpkin Cream CHEESECAKE

FREE OF: CORN, GRAINS, PEANUTS, SEEDS, YEAST

YIELD: 12 SLICES

SPICY GINGER CRUST *(can be prepared up to 1 day in advance)*

- **1 cup almonds, toasted** (see sidebar, page 16) **and cooled**
- **¾ cup pecans, toasted** (see sidebar, page 16) **and cooled**
- **2 tablespoons ground ginger**
- **½ teaspoon ground cinnamon**
- **¼ plus ⅛ teaspoon ground cloves**
- **¼ teaspoon fine sea salt**
- **¾ cup pitted soft honey dates** (see page 14)
- **1 tablespoon finely chopped candied ginger**

PUMPKIN CREAM FILLING

- **2½ cups raw cashews**
- **½ cup agave nectar**
- **¼ cup freshly squeezed lemon juice**
- **2 tablespoons nondairy milk**
- **1¾ cups mashed cooked or canned pumpkin**
- **2 teaspoons ground cinnamon**
- **2 teaspoons vanilla extract**
- **½ teaspoon ground nutmeg**
- **½ teaspoon fine sea salt**

To make the crust, lightly oil a 9-inch springform pan. If you don't have a springform pan, line a 9-inch round pan with aluminum foil; you can use the foil to easily remove the cheesecake from the pan once it has set.

Put the almonds, pecans, ground ginger, cinnamon, cloves, and salt in a food processor. Pulse until the nuts are coarsely chopped. Add the dates and candied ginger. Process until the ingredients begin to stick together, about 3 minutes. The almonds and pecans will be finely ground and the dates smooth. To test, squeeze a small amount of the mixture in your hand. If it doesn't stick together, pulse the mixture a few more times, being careful not to overprocess it. If it's not coming together, add 1 or 2 additional dates.

Scrape the mixture into the prepared pan using a rubber spatula, pressing it evenly on just the bottom of the pan with your fingers to form a crust. Put the crust in the freezer.

To make the filling, put the cashews in the food processor. Process on high speed until the cashews are finely ground and starting to stick together. Add the agave nectar, lemon juice, and nondairy milk. Process until completely smooth, stopping occasionally to scrape down the work bowl if necessary. Processing can take up to 15 minutes, depending on the strength of the food processor. Add the pumpkin, cinnamon, vanilla extract, nutmeg, salt, and cloves. Process until well combined. The heat from the motor should slightly warm the mixture, which is good; otherwise, when you add the coconut oil, it will harden. With the food processor running, add the coconut oil in a thin stream and process until smooth.

Per slice: 466 calories, 8 g protein, 36 g fat (11 g sat), 33 g carbohydrates, 143 mg sodium, 40 mg calcium, 4 g fiber

⅛ teaspoon ground cloves

½ cup coconut oil, melted

CANDIED PECAN TOPPING

¾ cup pecans, toasted (see sidebar, page 16) **and cooled**

1½ tablespoons light agave nectar

¼ teaspoon ground cinnamon

¼ teaspoon ground ginger

To fill the crust, remove the crust from the freezer. Spread the filling evenly in the crust using a rubber spatula, smoothing the top. Put the cheesecake in the freezer.

To make the topping, put the pecans in a large skillet over medium heat. Stir in the agave nectar, cinnamon, and ginger until the almonds are coated. Cook, stirring often, until bubbling and fragrant, 2 to 3 minutes. Transfer to a cutting board. Let cool completely.

Chop the pecans coarsely. Remove the cheesecake from the freezer. The surface of the filling should be firm enough to support the topping, which should not sink into the filling. If the filling isn't firm enough, put the cheesecake back in the freezer for 15 minutes longer. Sprinkle the topping over the filling, pushing down lightly.

Refrigerate, but don't freeze, the cheesecake for 12 hours before serving. To serve, remove the cheesecake from the pan and transfer it to a serving dish. Serve cold.

Tarts of All Sizes

Simplicity is the ultimate sophistication.
LEONARDO DA VINCI, ARTIST

See Raspberry Crumble Tart, page 62.

Tarts offer both simplicity and decadence in a singular dessert, making them the perfect finish for a dinner party or a casual brunch. Here you'll find a veritable smorgasbord of tarts, from all sorts of fruit tarts to a tart inspired by a favorite childhood sandwich—and, of course, a rendition of those popular pecan-caramel chocolate turtles.

THE TRUTH ABOUT TARTS

Tarts may look elegant, but making them requires no fancy skills. Most of my tart recipes call for easy-to-prepare fillings and press-into-the-pan crusts, although some require rolling out the dough. Whether they are rolled out or pressed into the pan, crusts turn out best when made from cold ingredients. And tarts are easier to make if you have certain kitchen tools. These tips will help you serve up tarts with flair:

- When making a pastry crust, follow the tips in Pies (page 28) for the best results. Use cold ingredients to avoid dense, tough crusts.
- When making a crust that's pressed into the pan, use your fingers or a tart tamper (see page 25) to press the crust evenly, paying particular attention to the area where the sides and the bottom of the pan meet.
- Tart pans come in a variety of shapes and sizes; my recipes use a 9½-inch round tart pan, which is the most common size.
- If you purchase a new tart pan, look for a metal pan with fluted edges and a removable bottom. With one or two pans like that, you'll be able to create tarts that will be easy to slice—and they'll look like they came from a fancy bake shop.

Storing Tarts and Troubleshooting

Refer to page 31 for details on storing tarts and table 4, page 31, for troubleshooting techniques.

Simplicity at its best, this tart comes together in a matter of minutes. It's the perfect showpiece to highlight raspberries at the peak of their season.

Raspberry CRUMBLE TART

FREE OF: NUTS, PEANUTS, SEEDS, YEAST

YIELD: 10 SLICES

1½ cups sorghum flour
½ cup millet flour
½ cup arrowroot starch
1¼ teaspoons xanthan gum
½ teaspoon fine sea salt
1 cup vegan buttery spread
⅔ cup plus 1 tablespoon unrefined cane sugar
1½ teaspoons vanilla extract
Finely grated zest of 1 small lime
2½ cups fresh raspberries

Position an oven rack in the middle of the oven. Preheat the oven to 350 degrees F. Lightly oil a 9½-inch tart pan with a removable bottom.

Put the sorghum flour, millet flour, arrowroot starch, xanthan gum, and salt in a large bowl. Stir with a dry whisk to combine.

Put the buttery spread, ⅔ cup of the sugar, and the vanilla extract in the bowl of a stand mixer or a large bowl. Turn the stand mixer or a hand mixer on medium-low speed and beat until well combined.

Turn the mixer to low speed. Gradually add the flour mixture, beating just until a soft dough forms. Scoop out about 1½ cups of the mixture to use for the topping and put it in a small bowl; refrigerate the topping. Press the remaining mixture evenly into the bottom and up the sides of the prepared pan to form a crust. Prick the crust with a fork about twenty times. Bake on the middle rack for 20 minutes, until firm but not brown.

Put the remaining tablespoon of sugar and the lime zest in a small bowl. Stir until well combined.

Evenly distribute the raspberries on top of the crust. Sprinkle with the sugar mixture. Remove the topping from the refrigerator and sprinkle it over the raspberries, gently squeezing the topping so it forms small clumps.

Bake for 32 to 38 minutes, until the raspberries are bubbling and the edges of the crust and the topping have just started to turn golden. Let cool to room temperature before serving.

Per slice: 352 calories, 3 g protein, 19 g fat (5 g sat), 39 g carbohydrates, 274 mg sodium, 8 mg calcium, 4 g fiber

All of my cookbooks include a recipe featuring peanut butter and jam, one of my favorite combinations since childhood. Here, in-season strawberries and salted peanuts add to the flavor intensity, which deepens if the tart is served the day after it's made. This tart is equally delicious warm, at room temperature, or chilled.

Peanut Butter AND JAM TART

FREE OF: NUTS, SEEDS, YEAST

YIELD: 12 SLICES

PEANUT BUTTER CRUST AND TOPPING

1¼ cups sorghum flour

½ cup teff flour

½ cup tapioca flour

1 teaspoon xanthan gum

¾ teaspoon baking powder

⅛ teaspoon fine sea salt

1 cup creamy natural peanut butter

¾ cup vegan buttery spread

¾ cup confectioners' sugar, sifted

⅓ cup unrefined cane sugar

1 teaspoon vanilla extract

3 tablespoons unsweetened nondairy milk, plus more as needed

⅓ cup salted peanuts

STRAWBERRY JAM FILLING

4½ cups sliced strawberries, about ¼ inch thick

¼ cup unrefined cane sugar

2 teaspoons freshly squeezed lemon juice

2½ tablespoons tapioca flour

To make the crust and topping, lightly oil a 9½-inch tart pan with a removable bottom. Put the sorghum flour, teff flour, tapioca flour, xanthan gum, baking powder, and salt in a medium bowl. Stir with a dry whisk until well combined.

Put the peanut butter, buttery spread, confectioners' sugar, sugar, and vanilla extract in the bowl of a stand mixer or a large bowl. Turn the stand mixer or a hand mixer on medium-low speed and beat until well combined. Add the nondairy milk and the flour mixture. Beat until smooth, adding additional nondairy milk as needed to create a texture similar to cookie dough.

Set aside one-third of the mixture for the topping. Press the remaining mixture evenly into the bottom and up the sides of the prepared pan to form a crust. Refrigerate both the crust and the topping for 20 minutes.

To make the filling, put the strawberries, sugar, and lemon juice in a medium bowl and stir gently to combine. Add the tapioca flour and stir until the strawberries are coated.

To fill and bake the tart, position an oven rack in the lower third of the oven. Preheat the oven to 350 degrees F.

Remove the crust from the refrigerator. Prick the crust with a fork about twenty times. Spoon the filling into the crust using a slotted spoon to avoid any juices. Sprinkle the topping over the strawberries, gently squeezing the topping so it forms small clumps. Sprinkle the peanuts over the topping, pressing them down lightly.

Bake in the lower third of the oven for 40 to 50 minutes, until the strawberries are bubbling and the edges of the crust and the topping have just started to turn golden. Let cool to room temperature before serving.

Per slice: 427 calories, 8 g protein, 23 g fat (5 g sat), 46 g carbohydrates, 134 mg sodium, 28 mg calcium, 5 g fiber

Fans of turtle-inspired treats will recognize this time-honored combination of decadent chocolate, salty caramel, and toasted pecans. Yeah, I'll leave it at that.

CHOCOLATE-CARAMEL-PECAN Tart

FREE OF: PEANUTS, SEEDS, YEAST

YIELD: 10 SLICES

COCOA SHORTBREAD CRUST

¾ cup sorghum flour

½ cup confectioners' sugar, sifted

½ cup natural unsweetened cocoa powder, sifted

¼ cup arrowroot starch

¾ teaspoon xanthan gum

⅛ teaspoon fine sea salt

10 tablespoons vegan buttery spread

CARAMEL PECAN FILLING

1 cup plus 1 tablespoon roasted creamy cashew butter

¼ cup agave nectar

¼ cup pure maple syrup

1 teaspoon blackstrap molasses

¾ teaspoon fine sea salt

¼ cup unsweetened nondairy milk

2 teaspoons arrowroot starch

½ teaspoon vanilla extract

1⅓ cups pecan halves, toasted (see sidebar, page 16)

CHOCOLATE TOPPING

½ cup nondairy semisweet chocolate chips

1 tablespoon nondairy milk

Per slice: 559 calories, 9 g protein, 40 g fat (10 g sat), 48 g carbohydrates, 503 mg sodium, 48 mg calcium, 5 g fiber

To make the crust, lightly oil a 9½-inch tart pan with a removable bottom. Put the sorghum flour, confectioners' sugar, cocoa powder, arrowroot starch, xanthan gum, and salt in a food processor. Pulse about ten times until well combined. Add the buttery spread. Pulse until the mixture begins to stick together and form clumps. To test, squeeze a small amount of the mixture in your hand. If it doesn't stick together, pulse the mixture a few more times, being careful not to overprocess it. Press the mixture evenly into the bottom and up the sides of the prepared pan to form a crust. Prick the crust with a fork about twenty times. Put the crust in the freezer for 45 minutes.

After the crust has been in the freezer for 30 minutes, position an oven rack in the middle of the oven. Preheat the oven to 350 degrees F. Remove the crust from the freezer. Bake on the middle rack for 25 to 30 minutes, until firm to the touch and no longer wet. Let cool completely before filling.

To make the filling, put the cashew butter, agave nectar, maple syrup, blackstrap molasses, and salt in a small saucepan. Cook over medium heat, stirring occasionally, until the mixture begins to bubble, about 2 minutes. Put the nondairy milk, arrowroot starch, and vanilla extract in a small bowl and whisk until smooth. Pour the nondairy milk mixture into the cashew mixture and stir until well combined. Cook over medium heat, stirring occasionally, for 1 minute, until creamy, thick, and smooth. Remove from the heat and stir in the pecans.

To fill the tart, spread the filling evenly in the cooled crust using a rubber spatula, smoothing the top. Let cool completely.

To make the topping, melt the chocolate chips with the nondairy milk using the microwave or stove-top method (see page 20). Drizzle the topping over the filling, then refrigerate the pie until the topping has set. Serve cold or at room temperature.

Salty pistachios and sweet, dried cherries are colorful and complementary companions in a silky chocolate ganache enveloped in a flaky shortbread crust. The red and green hues in this decadent tart make it perfect for entertaining around the holidays.

Pistachio-Cherry GANACHE TART

FREE OF: PEANUTS, SEEDS, YEAST

YIELD: 10 SLICES

SHORTBREAD CRUST

1 cup sorghum flour

⅓ cup confectioners' sugar, sifted

¼ cup arrowroot starch

¼ cup quinoa flour

¾ teaspoon xanthan gum

⅛ teaspoon fine sea salt

10 tablespoons vegan buttery spread

PISTACHIO-CHERRY GANACHE FILLING

1¾ cups nondairy semisweet chocolate chips

1 cup canned full-fat coconut milk, shaken

¾ cup salted dry-roasted pistachio nuts

½ cup plus 2 tablespoons dried cherries

Flaky sea salt or pink Himalayan salt, for sprinkling

To make the crust, lightly oil a 9½-inch tart pan with a removable bottom. Put the sorghum flour, confectioners' sugar, arrowroot starch, quinoa flour, xanthan gum, and salt in a food processor. Pulse about ten times until well combined. Add the buttery spread and pulse until the mixture begins to stick together and form clumps. To test, squeeze a small amount of the mixture in your hand. If it doesn't stick together, pulse the mixture a few more times, being careful not to overprocess it. Press the mixture evenly into the bottom and up the sides of the prepared pan to form a crust. Prick the crust with a fork about twenty times. Put the crust in the freezer.

After the crust has been in the freezer for 40 minutes, position an oven rack in the lower third of the oven. Preheat the oven to 350 degrees F. Remove the crust from the freezer after the oven has been preheating for 8 minutes and bake the crust in the lower third of the oven for 23 to 28 minutes, until firm to the touch and no longer wet. Let cool completely before filling.

To make the filling, put the chocolate chips in a medium bowl. Pour the coconut milk into a small saucepan. Cook over medium-high heat just until the coconut milk starts to steam and pour the coconut milk over the chocolate chips. Let stand for 2 minutes, then stir until smooth. Stir in the pistachios and cherries until well distributed.

To fill the crust, spread the filling evenly in the cooled crust using a rubber spatula, smoothing the top. Put the tart in the freezer just until the top of the filling is slightly firm, about 15 minutes. Sprinkle with the salt. Refrigerate, but don't freeze, the tart for 4 hours before serving. Serve cold.

Per slice: 504 calories, 6 g protein, 32 g fat (15 g sat), 52 g carbohydrates, 139 mg sodium, 11 mg calcium, 5 g fiber

Loaded with toasted nuts, figs, apricots, and raisins, this tart is an attractive (and delicious) addition to any holiday table. The flavors become even more intense once the ingredients have a chance to meld, so baking the tart in advance is recommended.

Holiday FRUIT AND NUT TART

FREE OF: PEANUTS, SEEDS

YIELD: 10 SLICES

ORANGE-CINNAMON CRUST

1 cup sorghum flour

¼ cup tapioca flour, plus more for rolling

¼ cup quinoa flour

1 tablespoon unrefined cane sugar

1 tablespoon finely grated orange zest

¾ teaspoon xanthan gum

½ teaspoon ground cinnamon

½ teaspoon fine sea salt

½ cup vegan buttery spread, cut into ½-inch cubes and put in the freezer for 20 minutes

2 tablespoons ice water, plus more if needed

1 teaspoon cider vinegar

½ teaspoon vanilla extract

FRUIT AND NUT FILLING

½ cup walnut pieces, toasted (see sidebar, page 16)

½ cup pecan pieces, toasted (see sidebar, page 16)

½ cup almonds, toasted (see sidebar, page 16) **and coarsely chopped**

½ cup chopped unsulfured dried calimyrna figs

½ cup unsulfured dried apricots, halved

To make the crust, put a 12-inch square piece of waxed paper on a work surface. Lightly coat a 9½-inch tart pan with a removable bottom with vegan buttery spread.

Put the sorghum flour, tapioca flour, quinoa flour, sugar, orange zest, xanthan gum, cinnamon, and salt in a medium bowl, a food processor, or the bowl of a stand mixer and stir with a dry whisk to combine. Follow one of the methods on page 29 for making the dough, adding the buttery spread, water, vinegar, and vanilla extract as directed.

Lightly dust a rolling pin with tapioca flour and roll out the dough, forming a circle about 12 inches in diameter and ⅛ inch thick. Use the waxed paper to carefully invert the dough onto the pan. Leaving the waxed paper on, ease the dough into the pan, using your fingers to pat it into the bottom and up the sides of the pan to form a crust. The dough on the sides of the pan should be a little thicker than the dough on the bottom. Prick the crust with a fork about twenty times. Refrigerate the crust for 30 minutes.

To parbake the crust, position an oven rack in the middle of the oven. Preheat the oven to 400 degrees F. Remove the crust from the refrigerator and gently press a sheet of aluminum foil or parchment paper into it. Fill with pie weights, dried beans, or uncooked rice. Bake on the middle rack for 15 minutes. Carefully remove the foil and weights and bake the crust for 8 to 12 minutes longer, until dry to the touch. If the crust puffs up, gently press it down with a spatula. Let stand while preparing the filling.

To make the filling, put the walnuts, pecans, almonds, figs, apricots, raisins, and flaxseeds in a medium bowl. Stir to mix well. Put the maple syrup and buttery spread in a medium

Per slice: 401 calories, 6 g protein, 23 g fat (4 g sat), 47 g carbohydrates, 223 mg sodium, 64 mg calcium, 5 g fiber

- ½ cup raisins
- 2 tablespoons ground flaxseeds
- ½ cup pure maple syrup
- 2 tablespoons vegan buttery spread
- ½ cup unsweetened coconut milk beverage
- 1 tablespoon tapioca flour
- ¼ teaspoon vanilla extract
- ¼ teaspoon fine sea salt

saucepan. Bring to a boil over high heat and boil, stirring occasionally, for 2 minutes. While the maple syrup mixture is boiling, put the coconut milk beverage and tapioca flour in a small bowl and whisk until no lumps remain. After the maple syrup mixture has boiled, whisk the tapioca flour mixture into the maple syrup mixture. Cook, whisking constantly, until thickened, about 1 minute. Remove from the heat. Stir in the vanilla extract and salt. Scrape the maple syrup mixture into the nut mixture using a rubber spatula and stir until well combined.

To fill and bake the tart, spread the filling evenly in the crust using the rubber spatula, smoothing the top. Bake for 25 to 28 minutes, until the filling is bubbling and the edges of the crust are brown. Let cool completely before serving.

If you like carrot cake, you'll love this tart, which features carrot cake batter baked inside a toasted walnut crust, then topped with a sweet lemon glaze. It's especially nice served with Clementine Spice Ice Cream (page 125).

LEMON-GLAZED Carrot Cake Tart

FREE OF: LEGUMES, PEANUTS, YEAST

YIELD: 10 SLICES

TOASTED WALNUT CRUST

¾ cup sorghum flour

½ cup chopped walnuts, toasted (see sidebar, page 16) **and cooled**

¼ cup arrowroot starch

1 tablespoon unrefined cane sugar

¾ teaspoon xanthan gum

¼ teaspoon baking powder

¼ teaspoon fine sea salt

3 tablespoons coconut oil, melted

3 tablespoons unsweetened nondairy milk, plus more as needed

CARROT CAKE FILLING

½ cup unrefined cane sugar

⅓ cup pure maple syrup

3 tablespoons coconut oil, melted

2 tablespoons ground flaxseeds

½ teaspoon vanilla extract

⅓ cup teff flour

⅓ cup sorghum flour

1 tablespoon tapioca flour

1 teaspoon ground cinnamon

¾ teaspoon xanthan gum

½ teaspoon baking soda

To make the crust, position an oven rack in the middle of the oven. Preheat the oven to 350 degrees F. Lightly oil a 9½-inch tart pan with a removable bottom.

Put the sorghum flour, walnuts, arrowroot starch, sugar, xanthan gum, baking powder, and salt in a food processor. Pulse about ten times, until the walnuts are finely ground. Add the coconut oil and pulse until the oil is mixed throughout the flour mixture. Add the nondairy milk, a little at a time, just until the mixture begins to stick together and form clumps. To test, squeeze a small amount of the mixture in your hand. If it doesn't stick together, pulse a few more times, adding up to 1 tablespoon of additional nondairy milk as needed.

Press the mixture evenly into the bottom and up the sides of the prepared pan to form a crust. Prick the crust with a fork about twenty times. Bake on the middle rack for 5 minutes. Remove from the oven and let sit while preparing the filling.

To make the filling, put the sugar, maple syrup, coconut oil, flaxseeds, and vanilla extract in the bowl of a stand mixer or a large bowl. Turn the stand mixer or a hand mixer on medium speed and beat until well combined.

Put the teff flour, sorghum flour, tapioca flour, cinnamon, xanthan gum, baking soda, and salt in a small bowl and stir with a dry whisk to combine. Turn the mixer to low speed. Gradually add the flour mixture, mixing until just combined. Add the carrots, raisins, walnuts, and ginger and beat until well mixed.

To fill and bake the tart, spread the filling evenly in the crust using a rubber spatula, smoothing the top. Bake for 30

Per slice: 315 calories, 5 g protein, 13 g fat (4 g sat), 37 g carbohydrates, 120 mg sodium, 45 mg calcium, 4 g fiber

½ teaspoon fine sea salt

1½ cups grated carrots (see tip)

½ cup raisins

½ cup chopped walnuts or pecans, toasted (see sidebar, page 16)

1 tablespoon finely chopped candied ginger

LEMON GLAZE

¼ cup confectioners' sugar, sifted

1 teaspoon finely grated lemon zest

1 tablespoon full-fat coconut milk or nondairy milk, plus more as needed

to 40 minutes, until a toothpick inserted in the center of the filling comes out clean. Let cool for 1 hour before glazing.

To make the glaze, put the confectioners' sugar and lemon zest in a small bowl and stir until well combined. Stir in the coconut milk to make a thick glaze. Add up to 1 tablespoon of additional coconut milk as needed if the mixture is too thick to spread. Spread the glaze on the tart using a metal offset spatula. Let the glaze set before serving.

TIP: Use a box grater, not a food processor, to grate the carrots. Carrots grated in a food processor release excess moisture, which will make the filling too moist.

Butter tarts are a quintessential Canadian dessert, traditionally filled with butter, brown sugar, eggs, and sometimes raisins or pecans or both . . . not exactly gluten-free or allergy-friendly. But with a couple of tweaks, my homeland favorite surpasses the original. It's sure to become a standard in your baking rotation.

BETTER THAN BUTTER Tarts

FREE OF: NUTS, PEANUTS, SEEDS

YIELD: 10 TARTS

BUTTERY CRUSTS

¾ cup sorghum flour

¼ cup quinoa flour

¼ cup tapioca flour, plus more for forming or rolling the dough

1 tablespoon unrefined cane sugar

¾ teaspoon xanthan gum

¼ teaspoon fine sea salt

½ cup vegan buttery spread, cut into ½-inch cubes and put in the freezer for 20 minutes

2 tablespoons ice water, plus more if needed

2 teaspoons cider vinegar

BUTTERY FILLING

⅔ cup unrefined cane sugar

¼ cup vegan buttery spread

¼ cup nondairy milk

1 tablespoon ground flaxseeds

1 teaspoon vanilla extract

½ cup raisins

To make the crusts, lightly oil ten cups of a 12-cup muffin pan. Put the sorghum flour, quinoa flour, tapioca flour, sugar, xanthan gum, and salt in a medium bowl, a food processor, or the bowl of a stand mixer and stir with a dry whisk to combine. Follow one of the methods on page 29 for making the dough, adding the buttery spread, water, and vinegar as directed. Knead up to 1 tablespoon of additional water into the dough if needed to hold it together. Divide the dough into ten equal pieces. Roll each piece into a ball between the palms of your hands. Put one ball of dough in each of the ten muffin cups and press it using a tart tamper or your fingers. Press the dough up the sides until it is about ⅛ inch thick.

Alternatively, lightly dust a work surface with tapioca flour. Lightly dust a rolling pin with tapioca flour and roll out one of the balls of dough, forming a circle about 3 inches in diameter and ⅛ inch thick. Transfer the dough to a muffin cup using a pastry scraper or butter knife. Gently press the dough into the bottom and up the sides of the muffin cup to form a crust. If the dough cracks, patch it with your fingertips. Repeat until you have made all ten crusts. Put the crusts in the freezer for 30 minutes.

To make the filling, put the sugar, buttery spread, nondairy milk, flaxseeds, and vanilla extract in the bowl of a stand mixer or a medium bowl. Using the stand mixer or a hand mixer, beat on medium-high until well combined. The filling might appear to be separated, but that's normal.

Per tart: 264 calories, 2 g protein, 14 g fat (4 g sat), 33 g carbohydrates, 179 mg sodium, 9 mg calcium, 2 g fiber

To fill and bake the tarts, position an oven rack in the lower third of the oven. Preheat the oven to 375 degrees F.

Remove the crusts from the freezer. Divide the raisins among the crusts. Spoon the filling over the raisins. Bake for 18 to 22 minutes, until the filling is bubbling and the crust is lightly browned. Let cool for 20 minutes. Carefully remove the tarts from the pan and transfer them to a cooling rack. Let cool completely before serving.

Delicate and delicious, these distinctive tarts feature a shortbread crust filled with lemon pudding that is topped with a drizzle of homemade white chocolate. Be sure to zest the lemons before juicing them.

SHORTBREAD LEMON TARTS WITH White Chocolate Drizzle

FREE OF: NUTS, PEANUTS, SEEDS, YEAST

YIELD: 18 TARTS

SHORTBREAD CRUSTS *(can be prepared up to 1 day in advance)*

1 cup sorghum flour

⅓ cup confectioners' sugar, sifted

¼ cup arrowroot starch

¼ cup quinoa flour

1¼ teaspoons xanthan gum

⅛ teaspoon fine sea salt

10 tablespoons vegan buttery spread

Tapioca flour, for rolling

LEMON FILLING

1 tablespoon lemon zest

½ cup freshly squeezed lemon juice

¼ cup tapioca flour

2 tablespoons sorghum flour

1 cup nondairy milk

⅓ cup agave nectar

¼ cup water

⅛ teaspoon fine sea salt

Per tart: 176 calories, 1 g protein, 10 g fat (4 g sat), 20 g carbohydrates, 88 mg sodium, 7 mg calcium, 1 g fiber

To make the crusts, have two or three muffin pans with a total of eighteen muffin cups ready. Put the sorghum flour, confectioners' sugar, arrowroot starch, quinoa flour, xanthan gum, and salt in a food processor. Pulse about ten times until well combined. Add the buttery spread. Pulse until the mixture begins to stick together and form clumps. To test, squeeze a small amount of the mixture in your hand. If it doesn't stick together, pulse the mixture a few more times, being careful not to overprocess it.

Lightly flour a clean surface with tapioca flour. Transfer the dough to the surface. Lightly dust a rolling pin with tapioca flour and roll out the dough until it is about ⅛ inch thick. Cut the dough using a 3-inch round cookie cutter (see tips). Transfer the dough to a muffin cup using a pastry scraper or butter knife, gently pressing the dough into the bottom and halfway up the sides of the muffin cup with your fingers to form a crust. If the dough cracks, patch it with your fingertips. If the dough breaks, reroll it. Repeat with the remaining dough, rerolling scraps as needed, to form all eighteen crusts. (Important: The sides of each crust should extend no more than halfway up the sides of the muffin cup.) Prick each of the crusts with a fork twice. Put the crusts in the freezer for 30 minutes.

To bake the crusts, position an oven rack in the middle of the oven. Preheat the oven to 325 degrees F. Remove the crusts from the freezer and bake for 10 minutes. Use a spoon to press down any parts of the crusts that puffed up while baking. Bake for 4 to 8 minutes longer, until the crusts are dry and just starting to turn golden at the edges. Let cool completely in the pan.

To make the filling, put the lemon juice, tapioca flour, and sorghum flour in a small bowl and whisk until smooth. Put the nondairy milk, agave nectar, water, lemon zest, and salt in a medium saucepan and whisk to combine. Cook over medium-high heat, stirring occasionally, just until the mixture begins

WHITE CHOCOLATE TOPPING

2.3 ounces (65 grams) **cacao butter** (see tips)

2½ tablespoons nondairy milk

1 tablespoon agave nectar

½ teaspoon vanilla extract

⅛ teaspoon fine sea salt

3 tablespoons confectioners' sugar, sifted

to bubble. Add the lemon juice mixture, whisking constantly. Cook and whisk over medium heat until thickened, 1 to 2 minutes. The mixture should be thick enough to coat the back of a spoon. Remove from the heat and let cool for 10 minutes.

To fill the tarts, remove the cooled crusts from the pans and put them on a plate. Spoon the filling into the crusts until they are full. Refrigerate the tarts for 2 hours.

To make the topping, put about 1 inch of water in a small saucepan and bring it to a simmer over medium heat. Put a glass bowl inside the saucepan, making sure it doesn't touch the water but creates a seal with the saucepan to trap the steam produced by the simmering water. Put the cacao butter, nondairy milk, agave nectar, vanilla extract, and salt in the bowl. Cook until the cacao butter is completely melted, then whisk until all the ingredients are well combined. Add the confectioners' sugar and whisk until the mixture is smooth. Remove from the heat.

Fill a large bowl about halfway with ice cubes. Pour just enough cold water over the ice to cover it. Set a small glass bowl that can accommodate the cacao butter mixture on the ice cubes. Pour the cacao butter mixture into the bowl and whisk it slowly for about 2 minutes, until the mixture is opaque and starts to thicken.

Remove the tarts from the refrigerator. Drizzle the cacao mixture over the filling in each tart. Refrigerate for 1 hour before serving.

TIPS

- The best way to know if you have the correct amount of cocoa butter is to weigh it yourself. A scale is a useful and inexpensive investment for gluten-free bakers, and it can be especially helpful for flour substitutions (see table 2, page 11).
- If you don't have a 3-inch round cookie cutter, use the rim of a glass that measures about 3 inches in diameter.

A traditional Pennsylvania Dutch recipe, shoofly pie got its name because molasses, a main ingredient, attracts flies that have to be "shooed" away. A variation on the classic pie, these tarts combine a cinnamon-spiced crust, a sweet and gooey filling, and a cupcake-like topping.

Sticky Molasses SHOOFLY TARTS

FREE OF: NUTS, PEANUTS

YIELD: 12 TARTS

CINNAMON-TEFF PASTRY CRUSTS

¾ cup sorghum flour

¼ cup teff flour

¼ cup tapioca flour, plus more for rolling

1 tablespoon unrefined cane sugar

¾ teaspoon xanthan gum

¼ teaspoon plus ⅛ teaspoon ground cinnamon

¼ teaspoon fine sea salt

½ cup vegan buttery spread, cut into ½-inch cubes and put in the freezer for 20 minutes

2 tablespoons ice water, plus more if needed

1 teaspoon cider vinegar

CRUMB MIXTURE

½ cup sorghum flour

¼ cup unrefined cane sugar

⅛ teaspoon fine sea salt

2 tablespoons vegan buttery spread

To make the crusts, lightly oil the cups of a 12-cup muffin pan. Put the sorghum flour, teff flour, tapioca flour, sugar, xanthan gum, cinnamon, and salt in a medium bowl, a food processor, or the bowl of a stand mixer and stir with a dry whisk to combine. Follow one of the methods on page 29 for making the dough, adding the buttery spread, water, and vinegar as directed and forming a single disk. Divide the dough into twelve equal pieces. Roll each piece into a ball between the palms of your hands. To form the tart shells, put one piece of dough in a prepared muffin cup and use a tart tamper to press the dough into the cup to form a crust. Use your fingers to make the sides thinner, about ⅛ inch thick, if needed. Repeat until you have made all twelve crusts.

Alternatively, lightly dust a work surface with tapioca flour. Put a piece of dough on the surface. Lightly dust a rolling pin with tapioca flour and roll out the dough, forming a circle about 3 inches in diameter and ⅛ inch thick. Transfer the dough to a prepared muffin cup using a pastry scraper or butter knife, gently pressing the dough into the bottom and up the sides of the cup with your fingers. If the dough cracks, patch it with your fingertips. Repeat until you have made all twelve crusts. Put the crusts in the freezer for 30 minutes.

To make the crumb mixture, put the sorghum flour, sugar, and salt in a medium bowl and stir with a dry whisk to combine. Using a pastry blender or two knives, cut the buttery spread into the flour mixture until the mixture is crumbly (it won't be as moist as traditional crumb mixtures). Scoop out ⅓ cup of the mixture and reserve it for the topping.

Per tart: 228 calories, 2 g protein, 10 g fat (3 g sat), 33 g carbohydrates, 190 mg sodium, 51 mg calcium, 2 g fiber

MOLASSES FILLING

½ cup molasses

½ cup boiling water

2½ tablespoons blackstrap molasses

1 tablespoon ground flaxseeds

1 teaspoon vanilla extract

½ teaspoon baking soda

⅛ teaspoon fine sea salt

To make the filling, put the molasses, boiling water, blackstrap molasses, flaxseeds, and vanilla extract in a large bowl and whisk to combine. Stir in the baking soda and salt—the mixture will bubble and expand. Add the crumb mixture (except for the reserved ⅓ cup) and stir until well combined.

To fill and bake the tarts, after the crusts have been in the freezer for about 20 minutes, position an oven rack in the lower third of the oven. Preheat the oven to 400 degrees F.

Remove the crusts from the freezer. Divide the filling equally among the crusts, leaving about ¼ inch between the top of the filling and the edge of the crust because the filling will expand during baking. Sprinkle the reserved crumb mixture over the filling.

Bake in the lower third of the oven for 18 to 22 minutes, until the filling has puffed up and the crust is lightly browned. Let cool completely in the pan before serving; as the filling cools, it may sink, which is normal.

Just as convenient and portable as commercial toaster pastries, this homemade version is more flavorful but has less sugar. If you prefer to toast these pastries, reserve the glaze and spread the pastries with it after toasting. The jam filling recipe makes extra, and the leftovers can be stored in the refrigerator in a sealed jar for one week.

Blueberry TOASTER PASTRIES

FREE OF: NUTS, PEANUTS

YIELD: 8 PASTRIES

BLUEBERRY JAM FILLING

1½ cups fresh blueberries

2 tablespoons freshly squeezed lemon juice

2 tablespoons pure maple syrup

Pinch fine sea salt

3 tablespoons chia seeds

PASTRY CRUST

1 cup sorghum flour

¼ cup tapioca flour, plus more for rolling

¼ cup quinoa flour

1 tablespoon unrefined cane sugar

¾ teaspoon xanthan gum

¼ teaspoon fine sea salt

½ cup vegan buttery spread, cut into ½-inch cubes and put in the freezer for 20 minutes

2 tablespoons ice water, plus more if needed

1 teaspoon cider vinegar

Nondairy milk, for brushing

Unrefined cane sugar, for sprinkling

To make the filling, put the blueberries, lemon juice, maple syrup, and salt in a medium saucepan. Cook over medium heat, stirring occasionally, until the blueberries are juicy, bubbling, and soft enough to mash with a fork, about 10 minutes. Mash until smooth. Stir in the chia seeds with a spoon until well distributed. Let cool to room temperature. Refrigerate until cold, at least 2 hours.

To make the crust, line a baking sheet with parchment paper. Put the sorghum flour, tapioca flour, quinoa flour, sugar, xanthan gum, and salt in a medium bowl, a food processor, or the bowl of a stand mixer and stir with a dry whisk to combine. Follow one of the methods on page 29 for making the dough, adding the buttery spread, water, and vinegar as directed. Knead up to 1 tablespoon of additional water into the dough if needed to hold it together.

Divide the dough into two equal pieces. Lightly flour a clean surface with tapioca flour. Put one piece of the dough on the surface. Lightly dust a rolling pin with tapioca flour and roll out the dough, forming a rectangle about 8½ x 7½ inches. Trim the edges using a knife so they're straight on all four sides and cut the dough into eight equal rectangles.

To fill and bake the pastries, transfer one rectangle of dough to the prepared pan using a pastry scraper or butter knife. Spoon about 2 teaspoons of the filling onto the dough, spreading it down the middle of the rectangle and avoiding the edges. Repeat with the remaining dough and filling.

Roll and cut the second piece of dough into eight rectangles of the same size. Using a pastry knife or your fingers, carefully position a rectangle of dough on top of a filled rectangle. Press

Per pastry: 216 calories, 3 g protein, 13 g fat (3 g sat), 23 g carbohydrates, 172 mg sodium, 19 mg calcium, 3 g fiber

VANILLA GLAZE

¼ cup confectioners' sugar, sifted

1 teaspoon vanilla extract

1 teaspoon nondairy milk, plus more if needed

down lightly so the top is flat; however, don't press down so hard that the filling spreads to the edges. Press the tines of a fork around the edges of the dough to seal in the filling. Poke the top six times with a wooden skewer. Repeat with the remaining dough, making eight pastries. Put the pastries in the freezer for 30 minutes.

After the pastries have been in the freezer for about 20 minutes, preheat the oven to 400 degrees F. Position an oven rack in the lower third of the oven. Remove the pastries from the freezer. Brush with nondairy milk and sprinkle with sugar.

Bake in the lower third of the oven rack for 25 to 28 minutes, until golden on the edges (if you're using a dark pan, the pastries will bake much more quickly, so check them after 15 minutes). Let cool completely before glazing.

To make the glaze, put the confectioners' sugar in a small bowl. Add the vanilla extract and the nondairy milk and stir until well combined and smooth. The glaze should be just thin enough to spread. If it's not, stir in additional nondairy milk until the desired consistency is achieved. Use a pastry brush to coat the tops of the pastries. Let the glaze set completely before serving or storing.

TIP: If you plan to toast the pastries, forgo the glaze and store the pastries, covered, at room temperature. Pop a pastry in the toaster or toaster oven, then glaze as directed.

At their peak of ripeness, nectarines are spectacularly sweet and look lovely alongside fresh red currants. If you serve the galette when it is still warm, the tart flavor of the currants will be dominant. However, the flavors will meld as the galette cools.

NECTARINE AND RED CURRANT Galette

FREE OF: NUTS, PEANUTS, SEEDS

YIELD: 8 WEDGES

BUTTERY PASTRY CRUST *(Single)*

¾ cup sorghum flour

¼ cup quinoa flour

¼ cup tapioca flour, plus more for rolling

1 tablespoon unrefined cane sugar

¾ teaspoon xanthan gum

¼ teaspoon fine sea salt

½ cup vegan buttery spread, cut into ½-inch cubes and put in the freezer for 20 minutes

2 tablespoons ice water, plus more if needed

2 teaspoons cider vinegar

NECTARINE–RED CURRANT FILLING

2 cups unpeeled sliced nectarines, about ⅛ inch thick (about 3 nectarines)

2 tablespoons sorghum flour

1 pint fresh or frozen red currants, stemmed (1¾ cups to 2 cups)

⅓ cup unrefined cane sugar, plus more as desired

FINISHING TOUCHES

1 tablespoon nondairy milk

1 teaspoon unrefined cane sugar

To make the crust, put a 12-inch square piece of parchment paper on a work surface. Put the sorghum flour, quinoa flour, tapioca flour, sugar, xanthan gum, and salt in a medium bowl, a food processor, or the bowl of a stand mixer and stir with a dry whisk to combine. Follow one of the methods on page 29 for making the dough, adding the buttery spread, water, and vinegar as directed and forming a single disk.

Put the disk in the middle of the parchment paper. Lightly dust a rolling pin with tapioca flour and roll out the dough, forming a circle about 12 inches in diameter and ⅛ inch thick. (The dough should roll easily; if it's crumbly, sprinkle it with up to 1 tablespoon of additional water and knead the water into the dough.) Transfer the parchment paper with the dough directly onto a baking sheet.

To make the filling, put the nectarines and 1 tablespoon of the sorghum flour in a medium bowl and stir gently until well combined. Arrange the nectarines on top of the dough, slightly overlapping the slices and leaving a 2-inch border of dough. Put the currants, the remaining tablespoon of sorghum flour, and ⅓ cup of the sugar in a medium bowl and stir gently to combine. Taste the mixture, adding additional sugar if desired. Spoon the currants on top of the nectarines—there will be a lot, but they'll break down while baking.

To finish and bake the galette, use the parchment paper to help fold the edge of the dough over the edge of the filling, using your fingers to pleat the dough as you do so. Gently press the dough over the edge of the filling to keep it intact during baking. Refrigerate the galette for 30 minutes.

Position an oven rack in the lower third of the oven. Preheat the oven to 425 degrees F.

Per wedge: 266 calories, 3 g protein, 12 g fat (3 g sat), 38 g carbohydrates, 173 mg sodium, 11 mg calcium, 3 g fiber

Remove the galette from the refrigerator and brush the edge of the dough with the nondairy milk, then sprinkle the sugar over the nondairy milk on the edge of the dough. Bake in the lower third of the oven for 15 minutes. Decrease the oven temperature to 375 degrees F. Without waiting for the oven temperature to adjust, continue baking the galette for 45 to 50 minutes longer, until the crust is golden brown and the filling is soft and bubbling. Let cool in the pan for 2 hours before serving.

shine brightly in this galette with a cornmeal crust. For an extra flaky crust, use full-fat canned coconut milk for both the vegan buttermilk and finishing touches.

FLAKY Winter Persimmon GALETTE

FREE OF: NUTS, PEANUTS, SEEDS

YIELD: 12 WEDGES

CORNMEAL PASTRY CRUST

1 cup sorghum flour

½ cup tapioca flour, plus more for rolling

¼ cup stone-ground cornmeal

¼ cup quinoa flour

¼ cup unrefined cane sugar

1 teaspoon xanthan gum

¼ teaspoon fine sea salt

½ cup plus 1 tablespoon vegan buttery spread, cut into ½-inch cubes and put in the freezer for 20 minutes

⅓ cup vegan buttermilk (see sidebar, page 23) **or full-fat coconut milk, plus more if needed**

PERSIMMON FILLING

¼ cup pure maple syrup

1 teaspoon finely grated orange zest

2 tablespoons freshly squeezed orange juice

2 tablespoons tapioca flour

¾ teaspoon ground cinnamon

⅛ teaspoon fine sea salt

8 fuyu persimmons, peeled and sliced ⅛ inch thick

To make the crust, put the sorghum flour, tapioca flour, cornmeal, quinoa flour, sugar, xanthan gum, and salt in a large bowl and stir with a dry whisk to combine. Using a pastry blender or two knives, cut the buttery spread into the flour mixture until the texture resembles coarse crumbs; the pieces of buttery spread should be no larger than peas. Drizzle the vegan buttermilk into the flour mixture and mix with a fork just until the dough comes together, adding additional vegan buttermilk, 1 teaspoon at a time, if needed.

Put a 12-inch square piece of parchment paper on a work surface. Transfer the dough onto the parchment paper. Knead the dough two or three times until it fully comes together. Lightly dust a rolling pin with tapioca flour and roll out the dough, forming a large rectangle about ⅛ inch thick. Transfer the parchment paper with the dough directly onto a baking sheet. Refrigerate for 15 minutes.

To make the filling, put the maple syrup, orange zest, orange juice, tapioca flour, cinnamon, and salt in a medium bowl and whisk to combine. Gently stir in the persimmons until they are coated with the maple syrup mixture. Arrange the persimmons on top of the dough, letting them overlap slightly and leaving a 2-inch border of dough.

To finish and bake the galette, use the parchment paper to help fold the edge of the dough over the edge of the filling, using your fingers to pleat the dough as you do so. Gently press the dough over the edge of the filling to keep it intact during baking. Put the galette in the freezer for 15 minutes.

Per wedge: 291 calories, 3 g protein, 9 g fat (2 g sat), 51 g carbohydrates, 126 mg sodium, 18 mg calcium, 6 g fiber

FINISHING TOUCHES

1 tablespoon nondairy milk or full-fat coconut milk

1 teaspoon unrefined cane sugar

2 tablespoons freshly squeezed orange juice

1 tablespoon pure maple syrup

Position one oven rack on the lowest level and a second oven rack in the lower third of the oven. Preheat the oven to 425 degrees F.

Remove the galette from the freezer and brush the edge of the dough with the nondairy milk, then sprinkle the sugar over the nondairy milk on the edge of the dough. Bake on the lowest rack for 25 minutes. Transfer the galette to the lower third of the oven. Decrease the oven temperature to 375 degrees F. Without waiting for the oven temperature to adjust, bake for 40 to 50 minutes, until the crust is golden brown and the persimmons are soft and bubbling. Let stand for 5 minutes.

Put the 2 tablespoons of orange juice and 1 tablespoon of maple syrup in a small bowl and stir to combine. Brush the persimmons with the mixture. Let the galette cool for 2 hours before serving.

Cobblers, Crisps, and Other Fruit-Filled Desserts

People love cinnamon. It should be on tables in restaurants along with salt and pepper. Anytime someone says, "Ooh, this is so good—what's in it?" the answer invariably comes back, "Cinnamon." Cinnamon. Again and again.

JERRY SEINFELD, *SEINFELD*, EPISODE "THE DINNER PARTY"

See Strawberry-Rhubarb Snickerdoodle Cobbler, page 87.

Fruit is the main attraction in cobblers and other rustic, homestyle desserts, including buckles, crumbles, and grunts. All of these desserts are easy to put together and fill the air with their inviting scents while baking. These humble creations are best served warm with nondairy ice cream (page 118), which begins to melt the moment that heavenly match is made.

Storing and Reheating Fruit-Filled Desserts

After baking, let a fruit-filled dessert cool completely, then cover it tightly with plastic wrap. Store the dessert at room temperature for 1 day or in the refrigerator for 2 days. Although fruit-filled desserts taste best when eaten the day they're made, leftover servings can be warmed in the microwave for about 30 seconds. Alternatively, preheat the oven to 300 degrees F and bake for about 15 minutes, until warmed through.

NAME THAT FRUIT-FILLED DESSERT

So what's the difference between a crumble and a crisp? And what the heck is a grunt? Here's a crash course to help you identify what these fruit-filled desserts really are.

Buckle. Similar to a coffee cake, a buckle has a cake batter on the bottom, a middle layer of fruit, and, typically, a streusel topping. During baking, the fruit sinks to the bottom and the cake rises, causing the dessert to "buckle."

Cobbler. So named because its top layer resembles a cobbled road, a cobbler features a layer of fruit paired with a biscuit, muffin, or cookie-dough topping. The dessert is baked until the topping is golden and the fruit is bubbling.

Crisp. In a crisp, a layer of fruit is topped with oats or nuts and baked until the fruit is soft and bubbling. In lieu of oats, I use buckwheat cereal. "Crisp" and "crumble" (see below) are terms that are often used interchangeably.

Crumble. A crumble has a layer of fruit that is topped with streusel and baked until the fruit is soft and bubbling.

Grunt. Also known as a slump, a grunt is basically a cobbler made on the stove top, steamed instead of baked, with dumplings in place of biscuits. The name comes from the "grunting" noise of the bubbling fruit.

Pandowdy. In a pandowdy, a pastry crust is arranged in overlapping pieces on top of a fruit filling. Halfway through the baking time, the crust is pressed down so the fruit juices can bubble over it.

TABLE 5 Troubleshooting when making fruit-filled desserts

Problem	Possible causes and solutions
The fruit filling is too runny.	• Let the dessert come to room temperature before serving; the filling will thicken as the dessert cools. • If the fruit is particularly juicy, add 1 additional tablespoon of flour or starch to the fruit filling before baking. • Review the tips for selecting fruit (page 17) and using frozen fruit (page 18).
The biscuits in a cobbler or grunt are underbaked.	• Bake the dessert longer.
The biscuits in a cobbler or grunt are overbrowned.	• Tent the dessert with aluminum foil to prevent overbrowning or burning.

The combination of chocolate and raspberry is guaranteed to make you swoon. Fruity, chocolaty, and decadent, this cobbler is best served warm and topped with a scoop of Very Vanilla Ice Cream (page 122).

DOUBLE CHOCOLATE-RASPBERRY Cobbler

FREE OF: LEGUMES, NUTS, PEANUTS, SEEDS, YEAST

YIELD: 9 SERVINGS

CHOCOLATE-RASPBERRY FILLING

6 cups fresh or frozen raspberries

¼ cup tapioca flour

2 tablespoons agave nectar

½ cup nondairy semisweet chocolate chips

CHOCOLATE BISCUIT TOPPING

¾ cup sorghum flour

½ cup teff flour

¼ cup tapioca flour or arrowroot starch

¼ cup natural unsweetened cocoa powder, sifted

4 tablespoons unrefined cane sugar

2 teaspoons baking powder

1 teaspoon xanthan gum

3 tablespoons coconut oil, softened

2 tablespoons unsweetened applesauce

½ cup unsweetened nondairy milk, plus more if needed

3 tablespoons nondairy semisweet chocolate chips

To make the filling, put the raspberries, tapioca flour, and agave nectar in a 9-inch square glass baking dish. Stir until the raspberries are coated with the tapioca flour and agave nectar. Sprinkle with the chocolate chips.

To make the topping, put the sorghum flour, teff flour, tapioca flour, cocoa powder, 3 tablespoons of the sugar, and the baking powder and xanthan gum in a large bowl and stir with a dry whisk to combine. Add the coconut oil and applesauce. Use a pastry blender or two knives to cut the mixture until it resembles moist, coarse crumbs. Gradually stir the nondairy milk into the flour mixture, using just enough to form a smooth but not sticky dough. If the dough is too dry, sprinkle it with additional nondairy milk, a little at a time, and work it in.

To assemble, scoop out about 2 tablespoons of dough at a time and drop it onto the filling until the dough is completely used up and the filling is evenly but not fully covered. Sprinkle with the remaining tablespoon of sugar and the 3 tablespoons of chocolate chips.

To bake and serve, position an oven rack in the middle of the oven. Preheat the oven to 350 degrees F. Bake on the middle rack for 30 to 35 minutes, until the topping is firm and the filling is bubbling. Let stand for 15 minutes before serving. Serve warm directly from the dish.

Per serving: 301 calories, 5 g protein, 12 g fat (8 g sat), 48 g carbohydrates, 65 mg sodium, 70 mg calcium, 9 g fiber

The simplest of desserts—sweet cherries topped with a flaky, old-fashioned biscuit topping—comes together in minutes. Using defrosted frozen cherries saves the step of pitting fresh ones, and the rest of the recipe can be prepped while the oven preheats.

Sweet Cherry COBBLER

FREE OF: NUTS, PEANUTS, SEEDS

YIELD: 9 SERVINGS

CHERRY FILLING

5 heaping cups pitted fresh or defrosted frozen sweet cherries, well drained

3 tablespoons unrefined cane sugar (see tip)

2 tablespoons tapioca flour

1 tablespoon freshly squeezed lemon juice

⅛ teaspoon fine sea salt

CREAM BISCUIT TOPPING

⅓ cup sorghum flour

⅓ cup millet flour

⅓ cup tapioca flour

5 tablespoons unrefined cane sugar

1 teaspoon baking powder

½ teaspoon xanthan gum

¼ teaspoon baking soda

⅛ teaspoon fine sea salt

6 tablespoons full-fat canned coconut milk, plus more if needed

1 teaspoon vanilla extract

1 teaspoon cider vinegar

To make the filling, put the cherries, sugar, tapioca flour, lemon juice, and salt in a medium saucepan. Cook, stirring often, over medium heat until thick, about 5 minutes. Scrape the filling into an 8-inch square glass baking dish using a rubber spatula, smoothing the top.

To make the topping, put the sorghum flour, millet flour, tapioca flour, 4 tablespoons of the sugar, and the baking powder, xanthan gum, baking soda, and salt in a large bowl and stir with a dry whisk to combine. Put the coconut milk in a measuring cup and stir in the vanilla extract and vinegar until well combined. Gradually stir the coconut milk mixture into the flour mixture, using just enough to form a smooth but not sticky dough. If the dough is too dry, sprinkle it with more of the coconut milk mixture, a little at a time, and work it in.

To assemble, scoop out about 2 tablespoons of dough at a time and drop it onto the filling until the dough is completely used up and the filling is evenly but not fully covered. Sprinkle with the remaining tablespoon of sugar.

To bake and serve, position an oven rack in the middle of the oven. Preheat the oven to 400 degrees F. Bake on the middle rack for 35 to 45 minutes, until the topping is firm and lightly browned and the filling is bubbling. Let stand for 15 minutes before serving. Serve warm directly from the dish.

TIP: If the cherries aren't supersweet, add up to ⅓ cup of unrefined cane sugar to the filling to taste.

Per serving: 164 calories, 2 g protein, 2 g fat (1 g sat), 37 g carbohydrates, 136 mg sodium, 13 mg calcium, 3 g fiber

That soft, chewy cinnamon-sugar cookie that we all know and love—the snickerdoodle—makes its debut in cobbler form. The sweetness of the unique cookie crust perfectly complements the tartness of the classic strawberry-rhubarb filling. Plus, this sweet-tart flavor improves as the cobbler sits, so don't hesitate to dig into leftovers for some midnight noshing.

Strawberry-Rhubarb SNICKERDOODLE COBBLER

FREE OF: NUTS, PEANUTS, SEEDS, YEAST

YIELD: 9 SERVINGS

SNICKERDOODLE COOKIE CRUST

¾ cup confectioners' sugar, sifted
¾ cup sorghum flour
¼ cup quinoa flour
¼ cup tapioca flour, plus additional for rolling
½ teaspoon xanthan gum
¼ teaspoon baking powder
¼ teaspoon fine sea salt
6 tablespoons vegan buttery spread
1 tablespoon unsweetened nondairy milk, plus more if needed
½ teaspoon vanilla extract

STRAWBERRY-RHUBARB FILLING

4½ cups sliced strawberries, about ¼ inch thick
2¼ cups chopped rhubarb, ¼- to ½-inch cubes
¼ cup unrefined cane sugar
3 tablespoons sorghum flour
½ teaspoon finely grated lemon zest

CINNAMON-SUGAR TOPPING

1 tablespoon unsweetened nondairy milk
1 teaspoon unrefined cane sugar
½ teaspoon ground cinnamon

To make the crust, put the confectioners' sugar, sorghum flour, quinoa flour, tapioca flour, xanthan gum, baking powder, and salt in a food processor. Pulse about ten times to combine. Add the buttery spread and pulse until the mixture is crumbly. Add the nondairy milk and vanilla extract and process just until the mixture starts to come together, adding additional nondairy milk if needed to form the dough. The dough should be soft and a little sticky. Transfer the dough onto a large piece of plastic wrap and form it into a disk. Wrap the disk in the plastic wrap and refrigerate for 30 minutes.

To make the filling, put the strawberries, rhubarb, sugar, sorghum flour, and lemon zest in a medium bowl. Stir until the fruit is coated with the sugar and sorghum flour. Scrape the filling into a 9-inch deep-dish glass pie plate using a rubber spatula, smoothing the top.

To assemble, remove the dough from the refrigerator. Position an oven rack in the middle of the oven. Preheat the oven to 325 degrees F. Lightly flour a clean surface with tapioca flour. Unwrap the dough and put it on the surface. Lightly dust a rolling pin with tapioca flour and roll out the dough, forming a circle about 10 inches in diameter and ⅛ to ¼ inch thick. Carefully invert the dough onto the filling and tuck in the edges.

To make the topping, brush the dough with the nondairy milk. Sprinkle with the sugar and cinnamon. Cut eight slits in the dough using a sharp knife.

To bake and serve, bake on the middle rack for 30 to 35 minutes, just until the topping is starting to turn golden around the edges. Don't overbake. Let cool for 4 hours before serving. Serve warm or at room temperature directly from the dish.

Per serving: 237 calories, 3 g protein, 8 g fat (2 g sat), 37 g carbohydrates, 139 mg sodium, 12 mg calcium, 3 g fiber

Besides being a fun word to pronounce, a pandowdy is a rustic, homey dessert inspired by deep-dish pie. Instead of cutting a slice, scoop out a generous serving. In this version, spicy cardamom highlights sweet pears; however, if you find the flavor of cardamom too intense, use cinnamon instead.

PEAR-CARDAMOM Pandowdy

FREE OF: NUTS, PEANUTS, SEEDS, YEAST

YIELD: 9 SERVINGS

FLAKY PASTRY

¾ cup sorghum flour

¼ cup quinoa flour

¼ cup tapioca flour, plus more for rolling

¾ teaspoon xanthan gum

¼ teaspoon fine sea salt

6 tablespoons vegan buttery spread, cut into ½-inch cubes and put in the freezer for 20 minutes

2 tablespoons coconut oil, cut into ½-inch cubes and put in the freezer for 20 minutes

2 tablespoons ice water

PEAR-CARDAMOM FILLING

6 unpeeled pears, halved, cored, and sliced ⅛ inch thick

½ cup freshly squeezed orange juice

2 tablespoons freshly squeezed lemon juice

1 teaspoon vanilla extract

⅓ cup unrefined cane sugar

3 tablespoons sorghum flour

1½ teaspoons ground cardamom or ground cinnamon

½ teaspoon fine sea salt

To make the pastry, put the sorghum flour, quinoa flour, tapioca flour, xanthan gum, and salt in a food processor and pulse about ten times to combine. Add the buttery spread and coconut oil and pulse six to eight times until they break down into pea-sized clumps and are well distributed throughout the flour mixture. Add the water and process just until the mixture starts to stick together in clumps. To test, squeeze a small amount of the mixture in your hand. If it doesn't stick together, pulse the mixture a few more times, being careful not to overprocess it.

Put a 12-inch piece of waxed paper on a cutting board. Using lightly floured hands, transfer the mixture onto the waxed paper and knead it to form a ball of dough. Lightly dust a rolling pin with tapioca flour and roll out the dough, forming a 10-inch square about ¼ inch thick. Leaving the rolled dough on the waxed paper and cutting board, put it in the freezer for 20 minutes. While the dough is in the freezer, prepare the filling.

To make the filling, put the pears, orange juice, lemon juice, and vanilla extract in a large bowl and stir until well combined. Add the sugar, sorghum flour, cardamom, and salt and stir until the pears are coated with the sugar and flour. Scrape the filling into a 9-inch square glass baking dish using a rubber spatula, smoothing the top.

To assemble, remove the dough from the freezer and cut it into 2-inch squares (the size and shape don't have to be exact) using a pastry wheel or knife. Arrange the dough in a patchwork pattern over the filling, leaving some spaces so the filling can show through. Brush the dough with the nondairy milk and sprinkle it with the sugar.

To bake and serve, position an oven rack in the middle of the oven. Preheat the oven to 400 degrees F. Bake on the middle

Per serving: 242 calories, 1 g protein, 11 g fat (5 g sat), 35 g carbohydrates, 258 mg sodium, 13 mg calcium, 4 g fiber

FINISHING TOUCHES

1 tablespoon unsweetened nondairy milk

1 tablespoon unrefined cane sugar

rack for about 30 minutes, until the filling begins to bubble and the crust is golden brown. Remove the pandowdy from the oven. Using a spoon, lightly press down portions of the crust so it's slightly submerged under the juicy filling.

Decrease the oven temperature to 375 degrees F. Without waiting for the oven temperature to adjust, return the pandowdy to the oven and continue baking for 35 to 45 minutes longer, until the juices are bubbling over the pastry and the pears are soft. Let cool for 30 minutes before serving. Serve warm directly from the dish.

A double dose of ginger highlights the sweetness of Italian prune plums in this crumble. Candied ginger is sweetened, though not crystallized, and can be found at most supermarkets.

Ginger-Plum CRUMBLE

FREE OF: NUTS, PEANUTS, SEEDS, YEAST

YIELD: 9 SERVINGS

CRUMBLE TOPPING

1 cup sorghum flour

⅓ cup tapioca flour

⅓ cup unrefined cane sugar

1 teaspoon baking powder

½ teaspoon finely grated lemon zest

½ cup vegan buttery spread, melted

GINGER-PLUM FILLING

2 heaping tablespoons finely chopped candied ginger

2 tablespoons unrefined cane sugar

2 tablespoons sorghum flour

¼ teaspoon ground ginger

6 cups quartered Italian prune plums (about 20 large plums)

To make the topping, put the sorghum flour, tapioca flour, sugar, baking powder, and lemon zest in a medium bowl and stir with a dry whisk to combine. Stir in the buttery spread until well combined. Refrigerate the topping while preparing the filling.

To make the filling, put the candied ginger, sugar, sorghum flour, and ground ginger in a medium bowl and stir with a dry whisk to combine. Stir in the plums until they're coated with the flour mixture. Scrape the filling into a 9-inch deep-dish glass pie plate using a rubber spatula, smoothing the top.

To assemble, remove the topping from the refrigerator. Use your fingers to gently squeeze the topping over the filling, forming small clumps, until the topping is used up and the filling is evenly covered.

To bake and serve, position an oven rack in the middle of the oven. Preheat the oven to 375 degrees F. Put the crumble on a baking sheet and bake on the middle rack for about 50 minutes, until the filling is soft and bubbling and the topping is golden brown. If necessary to prevent overbrowning, tent the crumble with foil after about 35 minutes. Let stand for 45 minutes before serving. Serve warm directly from the dish.

Per serving: 242 calories, 2 g protein, 10 g fat (3 g sat), 35 g carbohydrates, 121 mg sodium, 22 mg calcium, 2 g fiber

I love maple syrup, and I'm lucky enough that some of the best maple syrup in the world is made just down the road from my house. Here, maple syrup meets apples and pecans, making this crisp a fall classic that you'll want to serve all season long. Don't worry about peeling the apples—the skins soften as they're baked.

MAPLE-APPLE-PECAN Crisp

FREE OF: PEANUTS, SEEDS, YEAST

YIELD: 9 SERVINGS

MAPLE-APPLE FILLING

4 cups unpeeled sliced tart apples (see page 17), **about ⅛ inch thick** (about 3 large apples)

4 cups unpeeled sliced sweet apples (see page 17), **about ⅛ inch thick** (about 3 large apples)

½ cup raisins

¼ cup pure grade B maple syrup

2 tablespoons freshly squeezed lemon juice

2 tablespoons sorghum flour

PECAN CRISP TOPPING

¾ cup pecans

¾ cup sorghum flour

¼ cup arrowroot starch

1 teaspoon ground ginger

1 teaspoon ground cinnamon

¼ teaspoon fine sea salt

¼ cup pure grade B maple syrup

2 tablespoons vegan buttery spread

To make the filling, put the apples, raisins, maple syrup, and lemon juice in a large bowl and stir until well combined. Add the sorghum flour and stir until the apples are coated with the flour. Scrape the filling into a 9-inch square glass baking dish using a rubber spatula, smoothing the top.

To make the topping, put the pecans, sorghum flour, arrowroot starch, ginger, cinnamon, and salt in a food processor and pulse about ten times to combine. Add the maple syrup and buttery spread and process until the mixture begins to stick together and form small clumps. The pecans should be coarsely ground, and the topping should stick together if you press it.

To assemble, use your fingers to gently squeeze the topping over the filling, forming small clumps, until the topping is used up and the filling is evenly covered.

To bake and serve, position an oven rack in the middle of the oven. Preheat the oven to 375 degrees F. Bake on the middle rack for 35 to 45 minutes, until the filling is soft and bubbling. If necessary to prevent overbrowning, tent the crisp with foil after about 30 minutes. Let stand for 15 minutes before serving. Serve warm directly from the dish.

Per serving: 244 calories, 2 g protein, 9 g fat (1 g sat), 42 g carbohydrates, 89 mg sodium, 30 mg calcium, 5 g fiber

Peaches, blueberries, and raspberries are the delights of summer, and they're particularly delightful in this combination, which is accented with a crispy buckwheat topping. This crisp can be enjoyed for dessert or served at a late summer brunch.

PEACH AND BERRY Buckwheat Crisp

FREE OF: NUTS, PEANUTS, SEEDS, YEAST

YIELD: 9 SERVINGS

PEACH AND BERRY FILLING

5 cups unpeeled sliced peaches, about ½ inch thick (about 7 peaches)

1½ cups fresh blueberries

1½ cups fresh raspberries

¼ cup sorghum flour

3 tablespoons unrefined cane sugar

BUCKWHEAT CRISP TOPPING

1 cup uncooked creamy buckwheat cereal (see tip)

¾ cup sorghum flour

½ cup unrefined cane sugar

¼ cup arrowroot starch

¼ teaspoon fine sea salt

½ cup vegan buttery spread, cut into ½-inch cubes and chilled

To make the filling, put the peaches, blueberries, raspberries, sorghum flour, and sugar in a large bowl and stir until the fruit is well coated. Scrape the filling into a 9-inch square glass baking dish using a rubber spatula, smoothing the top.

To make the topping, put the buckwheat cereal, sorghum flour, sugar, arrowroot starch, and salt in a medium bowl and stir with a dry whisk to combine. Add the buttery spread. Use a pastry blender or two knives to cut the mixture until it resembles moist, coarse crumbs. Sprinkle the topping evenly over the filling.

To bake and serve, position an oven rack in the middle of the oven. Preheat the oven to 350 degrees F. Bake on the middle rack for 40 to 45 minutes, until the topping is golden brown and the filling is soft and bubbling. Let stand for 15 minutes before serving. Serve warm directly from the dish.

TIP: Creamy buckwheat is stone-ground cereal made from buckwheat groats. Bob's Red Mill manufactures a hot cereal under the name Creamy Buckwheat, and it works well in this recipe.

Per serving: 333 calories, 5 g protein, 11 g fat (3 g sat), 57 g carbohydrates, 152 mg sodium, 30 mg calcium, 6 g fiber

Prepared on the stove top, this traditional Nova Scotian dish features blueberries that are cooked until they're thickened, and then topped with a dumpling mixture that's steamed until tender. For added richness, I prefer to prepare the vegan buttermilk with canned coconut milk.

Nova Scotian BLUEBERRY GRUNT

FREE OF: LEGUMES, NUTS, PEANUTS, SEEDS

YIELD: 8 SERVINGS

BLUEBERRY MIXTURE

5 cups fresh or frozen blueberries (about 2 pints) (see tip for using frozen berries)

½ cup water

¼ cup unrefined cane sugar

1 tablespoon freshly squeezed lemon juice

DUMPLINGS

1 cup sorghum flour

½ cup arrowroot starch

½ cup millet flour or additional sorghum flour

¼ cup unrefined cane sugar

2 teaspoons baking powder

1 teaspoon xanthan gum

½ teaspoon baking soda

¼ teaspoon fine sea salt

2 tablespoons melted coconut oil

⅞ cup vegan buttermilk (see sidebar, page 23)

To make the blueberry mixture, put the blueberries, water, sugar, and lemon juice in an 11-inch skillet with a tight-fitting lid. Cook over medium heat, stirring occasionally, until the blueberries begin to soften and the mixture begins to thicken, 15 to 20 minutes. Make the dumplings while the blueberries are cooking.

To make the dumplings, put the sorghum flour, arrowroot starch, millet flour, sugar, baking powder, xanthan gum, baking soda, and salt in a medium bowl and stir with a dry whisk to combine. Stir in the coconut oil until the mixture is well combined and looks a bit crumbly. Gradually stir the vegan buttermilk into the flour mixture, starting with ¾ cup and using just enough for the mixture to hold together.

Decrease the heat to low, allowing the blueberries to simmer. Drop the dumpling mixture by tablespoonfuls (there should be about 16 in all) onto the blueberries. Cover the skillet with a tight-fitting lid. Cook without lifting the lid for 15 minutes. Remove the lid and let stand for about 20 minutes before serving.

To serve, spoon out one or two dumplings, putting them on a small plate or in a bowl, and surround the dumplings with blueberries. Top with a scoop of Very Vanilla Ice Cream (page 122), if desired. The grunt should be served the day it is made.

TIP: If using frozen berries, decrease the amount of water in the blueberry mixture to ¼ cup.

Per serving: 257 calories, 3 g protein, 5 g fat (4 g sat), 45 g carbohydrates, 151 mg sodium, 56 mg calcium, 4 g fiber

Traditional apple dumplings get a makeover in this recipe, with a caramel-like filling and a sweet apple cider sauce. For the best texture and sweetness, choose small Golden Delicious apples; if the apples are too large, you won't have the right ratio of filling to pastry.

Stuffed Apple Dumplings WITH CIDER SAUCE

FREE OF: PEANUTS, SEEDS

YIELD: 6 DUMPLINGS

DATE-CARAMEL FILLING *(can be prepared up to 1 day in advance)*

- **⅔ cup pitted soft honey dates** (see page 14)
- **1 tablespoon creamy roasted almond butter**
- **1½ teaspoons vanilla extract**
- **¾ teaspoon fine sea salt**
- **3 tablespoons apple cider, plus more as needed to reheat**

BUTTERMILK PASTRY CRUST

- **1¼ cups sorghum flour**
- **¼ cup quinoa flour**
- **¼ cup arrowroot starch**
- **¼ cup tapioca flour, plus more for rolling**
- **2 tablespoons unrefined cane sugar**
- **2 teaspoons baking powder**
- **1½ teaspoons xanthan gum**
- **¼ teaspoon fine sea salt**
- **⅔ cup vegan buttery spread, cut into ½ inch cubes and put in the freezer for 20 minutes**
- **½ cup cold vegan buttermilk** (see sidebar, page 23), **plus more if needed**

Per dumpling: 534 calories, 5 g protein, 22 g fat (6 g sat), 77 g carbohydrates, 591 mg sodium, 60 mg calcium, 7 g fiber

To make the filling, put the dates, almond butter, vanilla extract, and salt in a food processor and process until smooth. Add the apple cider, 1 tablespoon at a time, until a thick, creamy texture is achieved, stopping occasionally to scrape down the work bowl if necessary. If the filling is too dry, add up to 1 tablespoon of additional apple cider, 1 teaspoon at a time, until the desired consistency is achieved.

To make the pastry, put the sorghum flour, quinoa flour, arrowroot starch, tapioca flour, sugar, baking powder, xanthan gum, and salt in a medium bowl and stir with a dry whisk to combine. Add the buttery spread. Using a pastry blender or two knives, cut the buttery spread into the flour mixture until the texture resembles coarse crumbs; the pieces of buttery spread should be no larger than peas. Drizzle the vegan buttermilk into the flour mixture a little at a time and mix with a fork just until the dough comes together. If the dough is too dry, sprinkle it with additional vegan buttermilk, a little at a time, and work it in.

Put the dough on a clean work surface and knead it two or three times to form a ball. Flatten the ball into a disk and wrap it with plastic wrap. Refrigerate the disk while preparing the apples.

To coat and fill the apples, put the sorghum flour and cinnamon in a shallow bowl and stir until well combined. Use a small spoon to stuff each apple with the date-caramel filling, dividing the filling equally among the apples. Roll each apple in the flour mixture.

To assemble, lightly oil a glass baking dish, at least 9 inches square. Remove the dough from the refrigerator and put it on a lightly floured surface. Divide the dough into six equal portions. Lightly dust a rolling pin with tapioca flour and roll out one portion of the dough, forming a circle large enough to

APPLES

2 tablespoons sorghum flour

2 teaspoons ground cinnamon

6 small Golden Delicious apples, peeled and cored

FINISHING TOUCHES

2 teaspoons nondairy milk

1 tablespoon unrefined cane sugar

APPLE CIDER SAUCE

2½ cups apple cider

2 teaspoons sorghum flour

Pinch fine sea salt

encase an apple and about ⅛ inch thick. Put an apple in the center of the circle of dough. Bring up one side of the dough, using a pastry scraper to help if necessary, then bring up the opposite side, using your hands to squeeze the sides onto the apple. Repeat this process, bringing up the two remaining sides, and seal the pastry around the apple by pressing firmly with your hands and pinching the dough where it meets. Make sure the entire apple is covered securely with the dough. If the dough feels loose, carefully wrap your hands around it and give it a squeeze (the dough is forgiving, but because it's moist, it's also fragile). Put the apple in the prepared dish. Repeat with the remaining apples and dough. Brush the tops of the dough with the nondairy milk and sprinkle with the sugar.

To bake the dumplings, position one oven rack on the lowest level and a second oven rack in the middle of the oven. Preheat the oven to 450 degrees F. Bake on the lowest rack for 20 minutes. Transfer the dumplings to the middle rack and decrease the oven temperature to 400 degrees F. Without waiting for the oven temperature to adjust, continue baking the dumplings for 35 to 40 minutes longer, until the crust is golden and baked through and the apples are fork-tender. Let cool for about 20 minutes before serving. While the dumplings are baking, prepare the sauce.

To make the sauce, put the apple cider in a small saucepan and bring to a boil over high heat. Decrease the heat to medium-low and simmer until the apple cider has reduced to 1 cup, about 30 minutes. Pour about ¼ cup of the reduction into a small bowl. Add the sorghum flour and salt and whisk it into the reduction until smooth. Pour the flour mixture into the saucepan and whisk it into the remaining apple cider reduction until well combined. Increase the heat to medium and cook, stirring occasionally, until thickened, about 10 minutes.

To serve, scoop a dumpling onto a plate and spoon some of the sauce over the dumpling. Serve warm.

Store any leftover dumplings in the dish, loosely covered, at room temperature, without the sauce. Store the sauce in a covered container in the refrigerator. To reheat leftover dumplings, preheat the oven to 300 degrees F. Bake the dumplings until warmed through, about 15 minutes. Remove the sauce from the refrigerator. If the sauce is too thick, stir in additional apple cider until the desired consistency is achieved. Spoon the sauce over the dumplings, then bake until the sauce is warm, about 5 minutes longer.

Can't choose between cake and cobbler? You don't have to. A buckle combines the best of both worlds. Try to find the juiciest, plumpest blackberries when making this buckle, which works equally well as a dessert or brunch item.

Blackberry BUCKLE

FREE OF: NUTS, PEANUTS, SEEDS

YIELD: 9 SERVINGS

STREUSEL TOPPING

½ cup sorghum flour

⅓ cup unrefined cane sugar

¼ teaspoon ground cinnamon

⅛ teaspoon fine sea salt

3 tablespoons vegan buttery spread

BLACKBERRY CAKE

½ cup plus 1 tablespoon sorghum flour

¼ cup millet flour

¼ cup tapioca flour

1 teaspoon baking powder

½ teaspoon xanthan gum

¼ teaspoon baking soda

¼ teaspoon fine sea salt

2 teaspoons finely grated lemon zest

½ cup unrefined cane sugar

6 tablespoons vegan buttery spread

1½ teaspoons vanilla extract

½ cup plus 2 tablespoons vegan buttermilk (see sidebar, page 23)

3 cups fresh blackberries

To make the topping, put the sorghum flour, sugar, cinnamon, and salt in a small bowl and stir with a dry whisk to combine. Add the buttery spread. Use a pastry blender or two knives to cut the mixture until it resembles moist, coarse crumbs. Refrigerate the topping while preparing the cake.

To make the cake, position an oven rack in the lower third of the oven. Preheat the oven to 350 degrees F. Lightly oil a 9-inch deep-dish glass pie plate.

Put the sorghum flour, millet flour, tapioca flour, baking powder, xanthan gum, baking soda, and salt in a medium bowl and stir with a dry whisk to combine. Stir in the lemon zest until well combined. Put the sugar, buttery spread, and vanilla extract in the bowl of a stand mixer or a large bowl. Using the stand mixer or a hand mixer, beat on medium speed until smooth and well combined. Turn the mixer to low speed. Alternately add the flour mixture (in three additions) and the vegan buttermilk (in two additions), beginning and ending with the flour mixture, beating well after each addition. Turn off the mixer.

Spread the batter evenly into the prepared pie plate using a rubber spatula, smoothing the top. Sprinkle with the blackberries, pressing down lightly to create a single layer with a bit of overlap. Remove the topping from the refrigerator and sprinkle it over the blackberries. Bake on the lower third rack for 50 to 60 minutes, until lightly browned, and the blackberries are bubbling. Let cool for 30 minutes.

Serve warm or at room temperature directly from the dish.

Per serving: 267 calories, 2 g protein, 12 g fat (3 g sat), 38 g carbohydrates, 168 mg sodium, 35 mg calcium, 3 g fiber

Puddings, Pudding Cakes, and Layered Desserts

The key to successful baking is just to enjoy it.
Don't fuss, don't stress, and don't try to make it "perfect."

KATHLEEN KING, *TATE'S BAKE SHOP COOKBOOK*

See Black Forest Trifle, page 110.

Calling all messy bakers! Cake-topped puddings that beg to be paired with nondairy ice cream (page 118) and luscious layers upon layers in trifles and icebox cakes need no precision. These recipes feature complementary textures and flavors that will surely become fast favorites.

PUDDING CAKES

True to its name, a pudding cake combines the best of both worlds: a cake topping and a pudding-like bottom. The pudding is the saucy complement to the moist, delicious cake. To serve a pudding cake, you must scoop out—not slice—each portion.

When baked, a pudding cake is beautiful to behold; however, it's normal for this sweet concoction to look like a mess when it's ready to go in the oven. Follow the recipe method, and you'll find you have a huge puddle of liquid atop a thick cake batter. But don't fret! As it bakes, the cake rises through the liquid, which becomes the creamy pudding on the bottom. Be careful not to overbake a pudding cake, or the cake will absorb the pudding. Oh, and definitely serve it warm.

TRIFLES AND ICEBOX DESSERTS

Trifles and icebox desserts must be prepared in advance and chilled so the flavors can meld. The longer the dessert sits, the better—the flavor improves over time, and the varying tastes and textures come together to create a cohesive dessert. Many of the components can be or should be prepared one day in advance, making early morning the perfect time to assemble a dessert to be served after dinner.

Storing Puddings and Layered Desserts

For pudding cakes and puddings, cover leftovers with plastic wrap and store at room temperature for up to 1 day or in the refrigerator for up to 2 days. To reheat, follow the instructions on page 83.

For custards, trifles, and icebox desserts, cover leftovers with plastic wrap and store in the refrigerator for up to 4 days. Serve cold.

Chocolate pudding plus pumpkin pie? Welcome to bliss! The flavors in these easy-to-bake custards develop as they cool. Serve the custards at room temperature or cold. They're also great as leftovers the day after they're made.

CHOCOLATE-PUMPKIN Custards

FREE OF: CORN, LEGUMES, NUTS, PEANUTS, SEEDS

YIELD: 4 SERVINGS

1 cup nondairy semisweet chocolate chips

1¾ cups mashed cooked or canned pumpkin, at room temperature

1 tablespoon tapioca flour

1 teaspoon ground cinnamon

½ teaspoon ground ginger

½ teaspoon ground nutmeg

½ teaspoon vanilla extract

⅛ teaspoon fine sea salt

Position an oven rack in the middle of the oven. Preheat the oven to 350 degrees F. Lightly oil four 4-ounce ramekins.

Melt the chocolate chips using the microwave or stove-top method (see page 20). Add the pumpkin, tapioca flour, cinnamon, ginger, nutmeg, vanilla extract, and salt to the melted chocolate. Stir until well combined.

Divide the mixture evenly into the prepared ramekins using a rubber spatula, smoothing the tops. Put the ramekins on a baking sheet.

Bake on the middle rack for 20 to 25 minutes, until the tops are firm. Let cool for 15 minutes before serving.

Per serving: 347 calories, 5 g protein, 22 g fat (12 g sat), 43 g carbohydrates, 1 mg sodium, 18 mg calcium, 6 g fiber

This unique, not-too-sweet treat features creamy polenta studded with ripe strawberries and finished with Whipped Topping. For a little more decadence, serve with Maple Ice Cream (page 123) instead of the topping.

BAKED Strawberry-Polenta PUDDING

FREE OF: NUTS, PEANUTS, SEEDS

YIELD: 9 SERVINGS

- **2 cups sliced strawberries, about ½ inch thick**
- **½ cup plus 2 tablespoons unrefined cane sugar**
- **2½ cups unsweetened nondairy milk**
- **1 cup cornmeal**
- **2 tablespoons vegan buttery spread**
- **2½ teaspoons baking powder**
- **¼ teaspoon baking soda**
- **⅛ teaspoon fine sea salt**
- **1 cup vegan buttermilk** (see sidebar, page 23)
- **Pure maple syrup, for serving**
- **Whipped Topping** (page 24), **for serving** (start preparation 24 hours in advance)

Position an oven rack in the middle of the oven. Preheat the oven to 350 degrees F. Lightly oil an 8-inch square glass baking dish.

Put the strawberries and 2 tablespoons of the sugar in a medium bowl. Let sit while making the polenta.

Put the nondairy milk in a large saucepan (the saucepan must be large to allow the mixture to bubble and expand). Bring the nondairy milk to a boil over medium-high heat. Add the cornmeal in a steady stream, whisking constantly. Decrease the heat to medium-low and simmer, whisking constantly, for 5 minutes. Remove from the heat. Whisk in the buttery spread until it's melted. Then whisk in the remaining ½ cup of sugar and the baking powder, baking soda, and salt until well combined. Slowly pour in the vegan buttermilk, continuing to whisk until the mixture is smooth.

Drain the strawberries and reserve the juice. Stir the strawberries into the polenta. Scrape the mixture into the prepared dish with a rubber spatula, smoothing the top.

Bake on the middle rack for 35 to 40 minutes, until the edges are browned and the center is firm to the touch; the inside should seem to be unbaked. Let stand for about 1 hour to serve as a pudding or about 3 hours if you want a firmer dessert. Drizzle with the reserved strawberry juice and pure maple syrup and serve with Whipped Topping. This pudding is best enjoyed the day it's made.

Per serving: 151 calories, 1 g protein, 5 g fat (2 g sat), 27 g carbohydrates, 146 mg sodium, 91 mg calcium, 2 g fiber

Note: Analysis doesn't include maple syrup or Whipped Topping for serving.

Blueberries are at their peak in spring, and that's the perfect time to make this **pudding cake**. Serve it when you want a simple weeknight dessert or a sweet addition at brunch.

LEMON-BLUEBERRY Pudding Cake

FREE OF: LEGUMES, NUTS, PEANUTS, SEEDS, YEAST

YIELD: 9 SERVINGS

CAKE BATTER

2 heaping cups fresh blueberries

½ cup unrefined cane sugar

½ cup sorghum flour

¼ cup millet flour

¼ cup tapioca flour

1 teaspoon baking powder

½ teaspoon xanthan gum

¼ teaspoon baking soda

¼ teaspoon fine sea salt

2 tablespoons finely grated lemon zest

Juice of 1 lemon

½ cup unsweetened nondairy milk, plus more if needed

2 tablespoons coconut oil, melted

PUDDING MIXTURE

½ cup unrefined cane sugar

Juice of 1 lemon

1 tablespoon tapioca flour

1 cup boiling water

To make the cake, put the blueberries in an 8-inch square glass baking dish. Put the sugar, sorghum flour, millet flour, tapioca flour, baking powder, xanthan gum, baking soda, and salt in a large bowl and stir with a dry whisk to combine. Put the lemon juice in a liquid measuring cup. Add the nondairy milk. You should have ⅔ cup of total liquid; if necessary, add more nondairy milk. Add the coconut oil and the lemon zest and stir until well combined. Make a well in the center of the flour mixture. Pour the lemon juice mixture into the well and stir until combined to make a thick batter. Spread the batter evenly over the blueberries.

To make the pudding mixture, sprinkle the sugar over the cake batter. Put the lemon juice and tapioca flour in a small bowl and whisk until smooth. Pour the boiling water into a liquid measuring cup. Whisk the lemon juice mixture into the water. Slowly pour the pudding mixture over the batter, but do not stir the pudding mixture into the batter.

To bake, position an oven rack in the middle of the oven. Preheat the oven to 350 degrees F. Bake on the middle rack for 40 to 45 minutes, until the cake is golden brown and a toothpick inserted into the center of the cake comes out clean. Don't overbake or the cake will absorb the pudding, which should remain as a separate layer. Let cool for 20 minutes before serving. Serve warm.

Per serving: 186 calories, 2 g protein, 3 g fat (3 g sat), 39 g carbohydrates, 133 mg sodium, 26 mg calcium, 2 g fiber

This pudding cake is a lovely alternative to **pastry-based apple desserts**, and it comes together quickly and easily as the oven preheats. You don't even have to peel the apples—the skins just meld right into the cake.

Apple Cider PUDDING CAKE

FREE OF: NUTS, PEANUTS, SEEDS, YEAST

YIELD: 9 SERVINGS

CAKE BATTER

½ cup plus 1 tablespoon sorghum flour
¼ cup millet flour
¼ cup tapioca flour
2 teaspoons baking powder
1 teaspoon ground cinnamon
½ teaspoon ground ginger
½ teaspoon xanthan gum
¼ teaspoon ground nutmeg
¼ teaspoon baking soda
¼ teaspoon fine sea salt
⅔ cup unrefined cane sugar
½ cup nondairy milk
1½ tablespoons coconut oil, melted
1 teaspoon vanilla extract
2 cups unpeeled diced apples (see page 17), **about ¼ inch** (about 3 large apples)

PUDDING MIXTURE

1¼ cups apple cider
¼ cup unrefined cane sugar
1 teaspoon vanilla extract

STREUSEL MIXTURE

¼ cup sorghum flour
3 tablespoons unrefined cane sugar
2 tablespoons vegan buttery spread

To make the cake batter, lightly oil an 8-inch square glass baking dish. Put the sorghum flour, millet flour, tapioca flour, baking powder, cinnamon, ginger, xanthan gum, nutmeg, baking soda, and salt in a large bowl and stir with a dry whisk to combine. Put the sugar, nondairy milk, coconut oil, and vanilla extract in a medium bowl and whisk until well combined. Make a well in the center of the flour mixture. Pour the sugar mixture into the well and stir until combined to make a thick batter. Stir in the apples until they are coated with the batter; there will be more apples than batter. Spread the mixture evenly in the prepared dish using a rubber spatula, smoothing the top.

To make the pudding mixture, put the apple cider and sugar in a small saucepan and bring to a boil over high heat. Remove from the heat and stir in the vanilla extract. Slowly pour the pudding mixture over the cake batter, but do not stir the pudding mixture into the batter.

To bake, position an oven rack in the middle of the oven. Preheat the oven to 350 degrees F. Bake on the middle rack of the oven for 25 minutes. While the cake is baking, prepare the streusel.

To make the streusel mixture, put the sorghum flour and sugar in a small bowl and stir until combined. Add the buttery spread. Rub the buttery spread into the flour mixture using your fingers, until the mixture resembles coarse crumbs.

Remove the cake from the oven. Sprinkle with the streusel mixture, pressing it down lightly so it sticks to the cake. Bake for 15 to 18 minutes longer, until the cake and streusel are golden brown and a toothpick inserted into the center of the cake comes out clean. Don't overbake or the cake will absorb the pudding, which should remain as a separate layer. Let cool for 20 minutes before serving. Serve warm.

Per serving: 232 calories, 2 g protein, 6 g fat (3 g sat), 46 g carbohydrates, 124 mg sodium, 52 mg calcium, 2 g fiber

Coffee naturally enhances the flavor of chocolate, and the combination creates a mocha flavor that's hard to pass up. Brew some extra coffee one morning so you have an excuse to make this easy weeknight dessert.

Fudgy Mocha PUDDING CAKE

FREE OF: LEGUMES, NUTS, PEANUTS, SEEDS, YEAST

YIELD: 9 SERVINGS

CAKE BATTER

½ cup unrefined cane sugar

½ cup sorghum flour

¼ cup teff flour

¼ cup tapioca flour

¼ cup natural unsweetened cocoa powder, sifted

2 teaspoons baking powder

¾ teaspoon xanthan gum

¼ teaspoon fine sea salt

½ cup unsweetened nondairy milk, at room temperature

¼ cup coconut oil, melted

2 teaspoons vanilla extract

½ cup nondairy semisweet chocolate chips

PUDDING MIXTURE

½ cup unrefined cane sugar

¼ cup natural unsweetened cocoa powder, sifted

1½ cups brewed coffee

To make the cake batter, lightly oil a glass 8-inch square baking dish. Put the sugar, sorghum flour, teff flour, tapioca flour, cocoa powder, baking powder, xanthan gum, and salt in a large bowl and stir with a dry whisk to combine. Put the nondairy milk, coconut oil, and vanilla extract in a small bowl and stir until well combined. Make a well in the center of the flour mixture. Pour the nondairy milk mixture into the well and stir until combined to make a thick batter. Stir in the chocolate chips until evenly distributed. Spread the mixture evenly into the prepared dish using a rubber spatula, smoothing the top.

To make the pudding mixture, put the sugar and cocoa powder in a small bowl and stir with a dry whisk to combine. Sprinkle the mixture over the cake batter. Pour the coffee into a small saucepan and bring to a boil over high heat. Slowly pour the coffee over the batter. Do not stir.

To bake, position an oven rack in the middle of the oven. Preheat the oven to 350 degrees F. Bake on the middle rack for 30 to 35 minutes until the top of the cake is dry and firm. Don't overbake or the cake will absorb the pudding, which should remain as a separate layer. Let cool for 20 minutes before serving. Serve warm.

Per serving: 273 calories, 3 g protein, 12 g fat (8 g sat), 43 g carbohydrates, 129 mg sodium, 55 mg calcium, 4 g fiber

These individual pudding cakes feature a biscuit-like cake floating atop a gooey, maple syrup pudding. If you like pancakes generously doused in maple syrup, you'll love these mini cakes.

Mini Maple PUDDING CAKES

FREE OF: NUTS, PEANUTS, SEEDS, YEAST

YIELD: 4 MINI CAKES

CAKE BATTER

¾ cup sorghum flour

¼ cup unrefined cane sugar

2 tablespoons tapioca flour

1 teaspoon baking powder

¼ teaspoon xanthan gum

¼ teaspoon fine sea salt

½ cup plus 1 tablespoon nondairy milk

PUDDING MIXTURE

½ cup pure maple syrup

¼ cup nondairy milk

2 tablespoons water

1 tablespoon vegan buttery spread

To make the cake batter, lightly coat four 6-ounce ramekins with vegan buttery spread. Put the sorghum flour, sugar, tapioca flour, baking powder, xanthan gum, and salt in a medium bowl and stir with a dry whisk to combine. Pour the nondairy milk into the flour mixture and stir until combined. Divide the batter among the prepared ramekins using a rubber spatula, smoothing the tops evenly. Put the ramekins on a baking sheet.

To make the pudding mixture, put the maple syrup, nondairy milk, water, and buttery spread in a small saucepan over high heat. Whisk to combine. Once the mixture is steaming, remove it from the heat and carefully pour it into a liquid measuring cup (this will make it easier to pour over the batter). Slowly pour an equal amount of the mixture over the batter in each ramekin. Do not stir.

To bake, position an oven rack in the middle of the oven. Preheat the oven to 350 degrees F. Bake on the middle rack for 22 to 25 minutes, until the tops of the cakes are firm, the maple syrup is bubbling up the sides, and a toothpick inserted in the center of the cakes comes out clean. Don't overbake or the cakes will absorb the pudding, which should remain as a separate layer. Let cool for 20 minutes before serving.

Per ramekin: 286 calories, 3 g protein, 4 g fat (2 g sat), 61 g carbohydrates, 250 mg sodium, 89 mg calcium, 2 g fiber

If you're a fan of chocolate chip cookie dough, you'll count down the seconds until you can dig into these warm, gooey desserts. And here's some really good news: you can assemble and refrigerate these single servings in advance and bake one or more on demand for an impromptu dessert (see tip).

DEEP-DISH CHOCOLATE CHIP Cookie Bowls

FREE OF: NUTS, PEANUTS, SEEDS, YEAST

YIELD: 4 GENEROUS SERVINGS

⅔ cup unrefined cane sugar
½ cup vegan buttery spread
3 tablespoons nondairy milk
2 teaspoons vanilla extract
¾ cup plus 1 tablespoon sorghum flour
⅓ cup millet flour
¼ cup tapioca flour
1 teaspoon baking soda
½ teaspoon xanthan gum
¼ teaspoon fine sea salt
⅛ teaspoon baking powder
⅔ cup nondairy semisweet chocolate chips

Position an oven rack in the middle of the oven. Preheat the oven to 350 degrees F. Lightly oil four 6-ounce ramekins.

Put the sugar and buttery spread in the bowl of a stand mixer or a large bowl. Using the stand mixer or a hand mixer, beat on medium-high speed until smooth and fluffy, about 2 minutes. Add the nondairy milk and vanilla extract and beat until well combined.

Put the sorghum flour, millet flour, tapioca flour, baking soda, xanthan gum, salt, and baking powder in a medium bowl and stir with a dry whisk to combine.

Turn the mixer to low speed. Gradually add the flour mixture to the sugar mixture, beating until just combined. Turn off the mixer. Stir in the chocolate chips.

Divide the dough equally among the prepared ramekins, pressing it down evenly. Put the ramekins on a baking sheet. Bake on the middle rack for 18 to 20 minutes, until the top is golden brown but the middle is slightly underbaked. (It's normal for the cookie bowls to puff up while baking, and then the center will collapse).

Let cool for 20 minutes before serving. Serve warm; if desired, top each cookie bowl with a scoop of nondairy ice cream (page 118).

TIP: To make the cookie bowls in advance, prepare the recipe as directed. After pressing the dough into the ramekins, cover and refrigerate for up to 2 days. Remove from the refrigerator and let stand at room temperature while preheating the oven. If the cookie bowls are still very cold, they may need a few additional minutes of baking time.

Per bowl: 703 calories, 7 g protein, 37 g fat (15 g sat), 91 g carbohydrates, 663 mg sodium, 3 mg calcium, 6 g fiber

A refreshing late-summer dessert, this trifle combines ripe, juicy peaches and lemon pudding with sweet, moist cornbread and nondairy whipped cream. Be sure to start preparing the Whipped Topping twenty-four hours in advance.

SUMMERY PEACH Cornbread Trifle

FREE OF: NUTS, PEANUTS, SEEDS

YIELD: 12 SERVINGS

SWEET CORNBREAD *(can be prepared up to 1 day in advance)*

1¼ cups cornmeal

½ cup sorghum flour

½ cup arrowroot starch

1 tablespoon baking powder

1½ teaspoons xanthan gum

½ teaspoon fine sea salt

1½ cups vegan buttermilk (see sidebar, page 23)

¼ cup agave nectar

2 tablespoons plus 1 teaspoon coconut oil, melted

2 tablespoons unrefined cane sugar

1 teaspoon vanilla extract

LEMON PUDDING *(prepare at least 6 hours in advance)*

2 cups nondairy milk

⅓ cup agave nectar

¼ cup arrowroot starch

2 tablespoons sorghum flour

⅛ teaspoon fine sea salt

1 tablespoon lemon zest

½ cup freshly squeezed lemon juice

To make the cornbread, position an oven rack in the middle of the oven. Preheat the oven to 350 degrees F. Lightly oil a 9-inch square glass baking dish. Put the cornmeal, sorghum flour, arrowroot starch, baking powder, xanthan gum, and salt in a medium bowl and stir with a dry whisk to combine. Put the vegan buttermilk, agave nectar, coconut oil, sugar, and vanilla extract in a medium bowl and stir to combine. Pour the vegan buttermilk mixture into the flour mixture, stirring until just moistened. Spread the batter evenly in the prepared dish. Bake on the middle rack for 25 to 30 minutes, until a toothpick inserted in the center of the cornbread comes out clean. Let cool completely in the dish.

To make the pudding, put ¼ cup of the nondairy milk and the agave nectar, arrowroot starch, sorghum flour, and salt in a small bowl and whisk until smooth. Pour the remaining 1¾ cups of nondairy milk into a small saucepan and stir in the lemon zest and lemon juice. Bring to a simmer over medium heat. Pour about ¼ cup of the warm nondairy milk mixture into the agave nectar mixture and whisk until well combined. (This will help eliminate lumps). Whisk the agave nectar mixture into the remaining nondairy milk mixture in the saucepan. Cook over medium-low heat, whisking constantly, until thickened, about 2 minutes. Once the mixture is very thick, whisk briskly for 30 seconds and immediately remove from the heat. Scrape the pudding into a small bowl using a rubber spatula. Put a piece of plastic wrap or waxed paper directly on top of the pudding, pressing down lightly so the plastic wrap sticks to the pudding's surface to prevent a skin from forming. Let cool to room temperature, then refrigerate for 6 hours.

Per serving: 356 calories, 3 g protein, 17 g fat (14 g sat), 50 g carbohydrates, 204 mg sodium, 36 mg calcium, 4 g fiber

FINISHING TOUCHES

6 cups unpeeled sliced fresh peaches, about ½ inch thick (about 8 peaches)

About 2½ cups Whipped Topping (page 24; prepared and refrigerated until needed)

To assemble the trifle, invert the cornbread out of the pan and onto a cutting board. Cut the cornbread into ¾-inch cubes. Put about one-third of the cornbread in a trifle bowl or large serving bowl, at least 3 quarts in volume. Spread half the pudding over the cornbread using a metal offset spatula. Top with one-third of the peaches, followed by one-third of the Whipped Topping. Repeat the sequence with half the remaining cornbread, all the remaining pudding, half the remaining peaches, and half the remaining Whipped Topping. Finish the layers in this order: cornbread, Whipped Topping, and peaches.

Refrigerate for 6 hours before serving.

This trifle is definitely one of my favorites. Cookies replace the more traditional banana bread and mingle with chocolate pudding, fresh strawberry and banana slices, and nondairy whipped cream. Be sure to start preparing the Whipped Topping twenty-four hours in advance.

CHOCOLATE-STRAWBERRY Banana Bread Trifle

FREE OF: NUTS, PEANUTS, SEEDS

YIELD: 12 SERVINGS

BANANA BREAD COOKIES *(can be prepared up to 1 day in advance)*

- **¾ cup unrefined cane sugar**
- **6 tablespoons coconut oil, softened but not melted**
- **¼ teaspoon vanilla extract**
- **1¼ cups mashed ripe bananas** (about 2½ bananas)
- **1 teaspoon baking soda**
- **1¼ cups sorghum flour**
- **½ cup tapioca flour**
- **¼ cup quinoa flour**
- **¾ teaspoon xanthan gum**
- **½ teaspoon ground cinnamon**
- **¼ teaspoon baking powder**
- **⅛ teaspoon fine sea salt**
- **1 tablespoon nondairy milk**

To make the cookies, position an oven rack in the lower third of the oven. Preheat the oven to 350 degrees F. Line a baking sheet with parchment paper or a Silpat liner.

Put the sugar, coconut oil, and vanilla extract in the bowl of a stand mixer or a large bowl. Using the stand mixer or a hand mixer, beat on medium-high speed until smooth and creamy. Put the mashed banana in a small bowl and stir in the baking soda until well combined. Let stand for 2 minutes. Put the sorghum flour, tapioca flour, quinoa flour, xanthan gum, cinnamon, baking powder, and salt in a large bowl and stir with a dry whisk to combine. Add the banana mixture to the sugar mixture and beat on medium-high speed until well combined. Add the nondairy milk and beat until well mixed. Turn the mixer to low speed. Gradually add the flour mixture to the sugar mixture, beating until just combined. Turn off the mixer.

For each cookie, scoop out 3 tablespoons of dough and drop it onto the prepared baking sheet, pressing down lightly and smoothing if needed. Repeat with the remaining dough.

Bake in the lower third of the oven for 13 to 18 minutes, until golden brown. Let cool on the baking sheet for 5 minutes. Carefully remove the cookies from the baking sheet and transfer them to a cooling rack. Let cool completely.

Per serving: 483 calories, 5 g protein, 26 g fat (19 g sat), 65 g carbohydrates, 132 mg sodium, 40 mg calcium, 6 g fiber

CHOCOLATE PUDDING *(prepare at least 6 hours in advance)*

½ cup nondairy semisweet chocolate chips

2½ cups nondairy milk

½ cup unrefined cane sugar

½ cup natural unsweetened cocoa powder, sifted

¼ teaspoon fine sea salt

3 tablespoons tapioca flour

½ teaspoon vanilla extract

2 tablespoons agave nectar, if needed

FINISHING TOUCHES *(start preparation 24 hours in advance)*

4 cups sliced strawberries, about ½ inch thick

3 fresh but not overripe bananas, sliced about ½ inch thick

About 2½ cups Whipped Topping (page 24; prepared and refrigerated until needed)

To make the pudding, melt the chocolate chips using the microwave or stove-top method (see page 20). Put 2¼ cups of the nondairy milk and the sugar, cocoa powder, and salt in a medium saucepan and whisk until no lumps remain. Cook over medium-high heat, whisking occasionally, just until the mixture begins to bubble. Put the remaining ¼ cup of nondairy milk and the tapioca flour in a small bowl and whisk until no lumps remain. Add the tapioca flour mixture to the sugar mixture in the saucepan, whisking constantly. Cook over medium heat, stirring occasionally, until the mixture thickens and coats the back of a spoon, about 3 minutes. Scrape into a medium bowl using a rubber spatula. Add the melted chocolate and vanilla extract and whisk until well combined. Taste for sweetness; if desired, stir in the agave nectar, 1 tablespoon at a time. Put a piece of plastic wrap or waxed paper directly on top of the pudding, pressing down lightly so the plastic wrap sticks to the pudding's surface to prevent a skin from forming. Let cool to room temperature, then refrigerate for 8 hours.

To assemble the trifle, crumble the cookies into bite-sized pieces and put them in a medium bowl. Put about one-third of the crumbled cookies in a trifle bowl or large serving bowl, at least 3 quarts in volume. Spread one-third of the pudding over the cookies using a metal offset spatula (the pudding will be very thick). Top with one-third of the strawberries and one-third of the bananas, followed by one-third of the Whipped Topping. Repeat the sequence twice in the same order: cookies, pudding, strawberries, bananas, and Whipped Topping.

Refrigerate for 6 hours before serving.

TIP: Not a fan of strawberries or having trouble finding fresh ones? Fresh raspberries are a delicious alternative.

Chocolate cake, sour cherry filling, nondairy whipped cream, and a rich chocolate ganache join together in a trifle that is an homage to an old classic—Black Forest Cake. Be sure to start preparing the Whipped Topping twenty-four hours in advance.

Black Forest TRIFLE

FREE OF: NUTS, PEANUTS, SEEDS

YIELD: 12 SERVINGS

CHOCOLATE CAKE

1¼ cups sorghum flour

¾ cup natural unsweetened cocoa powder, sifted

½ cup teff flour

½ cup arrowroot starch

¼ cup tapioca flour

2 teaspoons baking soda

1½ teaspoons xanthan gum

½ teaspoon baking powder

¼ teaspoon fine sea salt

1¾ cups unrefined cane sugar

1 cup brewed coffee

1 cup cold water

6 tablespoons coconut oil, melted

2 tablespoons cider vinegar

2 teaspoons vanilla extract

CHERRY FILLING

6 cups unsweetened pitted fresh or defrosted sour cherries, well drained, juice reserved

½ cup unrefined cane sugar

¼ cup tapioca flour

To make the cake, position an oven rack in the middle of the oven. Preheat the oven to 350 degrees F. Lightly oil two 9-inch round baking pans. Sprinkle with cocoa powder, tapping out the excess.

Put the sorghum flour, cocoa powder, teff flour, arrowroot starch, tapioca flour, baking soda, xanthan gum, baking powder, and salt in a large bowl and stir with a dry whisk to combine. Put the sugar, coffee, water, coconut oil, vinegar, and vanilla extract in a medium bowl and whisk to combine. Make a well in the center of the flour mixture. Pour the sugar mixture into the well and stir until well mixed. Spread the batter in the prepared pans. Bake on the middle rack for 25 to 30 minutes, until a toothpick inserted in the center of each cake comes out clean and the cakes begin to pull away from the sides of the pans. Let the cakes cool in the pans for 10 minutes, then carefully remove the cakes from the pans and transfer them to a cooling rack. Let cool completely.

To make the filling, put the cherries in a medium saucepan. If using fresh cherries, cook over medium-high heat until the cherries begin to break down and are juicy. If using thawed frozen cherries, which will already be broken down, cook just until the cherries are juicy. Fresh and frozen cherries will yield different amounts of juice; cook until there's ½ to ⅔ cup of juice in the saucepan. If the frozen cherries don't produce that much juice, add the juice reserved from draining them. Bring the cherries to a boil. Put the sugar and tapioca flour in a small bowl and stir until well combined. Sprinkle the mixture over the cherries. Cook, stirring constantly, until thickened, about 2 minutes. Let cool to room temperature.

Per serving: 601 calories, 6 g protein, 30 g fat (22 g sat), 86 g carbohydrates, 280 mg sodium, 17 mg calcium, 6 g fiber

CHOCOLATE GANACHE

1¼ cups nondairy semisweet chocolate chips

¼ cup unsweetened nondairy milk

FINISHING TOUCHES

About 2½ cups Whipped Topping (page 24; prepared and refrigerated until needed)

To make the ganache, put the chocolate chips in a small bowl. Pour the nondairy milk into a small saucepan and cook over medium-high heat just until it starts to steam. Remove from the heat and pour over the chocolate chips. Let stand for 2 minutes, then stir until smooth. Let cool for 10 minutes.

To assemble the trifle, cut the cakes into ¾-inch cubes. Put about one-third of the cake in a trifle bowl or large serving bowl, at least 3 quarts in volume. Top with one-third of the filling, followed by one-third of the Whipped Topping. Drizzle with one-third of the ganache. Repeat the sequence twice in the same order: cake, filling, Whipped Topping, and ganache.

Refrigerate for 6 hours before serving.

This impressive five-layer trifle features a double dose of lemon, which shines in both the cake and the tangy sauce. Also featuring cranberries, a pecan crumble, and nondairy whipped cream, this combination is anything but ordinary. Be sure to zest the lemons before juicing them, and start preparing the Whipped Topping twenty-four hours in advance. For other advance-preparation ideas, see the tip (page 113).

Lemon-Cranberry Trifle WITH PECAN CRUMBLE

FREE OF: PEANUTS

YIELD: 12 SERVINGS

LEMON CAKE *(can be prepared up to 1 day in advance)*

¾ cup sorghum flour

⅔ cup millet flour

⅓ cup arrowroot starch

¼ cup tapioca flour

1¼ teaspoons baking powder

1 teaspoon xanthan gum

¾ teaspoon baking soda

½ teaspoon fine sea salt

1 cup unrefined cane sugar

7 tablespoons coconut oil, melted

2 tablespoons finely grated lemon zest

3 tablespoons freshly squeezed lemon juice

2 teaspoons ground flaxseeds

1 cup plus 2 tablespoons vegan buttermilk (see sidebar, page 23)

2 teaspoons cider vinegar

CRANBERRY FILLING *(can be prepared up to 1 day in advance)*

6 cups fresh or frozen cranberries

1 large sweet-tart apple (see page 17), **peeled and grated**

½ cup agave nectar, plus more if desired

To make the cake, position an oven rack in the middle of the oven. Preheat the oven to 350 degrees F. Lightly oil two 9-inch round baking pans, line them with parchment paper, and lightly oil the parchment paper.

Put the sorghum flour, millet flour, arrowroot starch, tapioca flour, baking powder, xanthan gum, baking soda, and salt in a medium bowl and stir with a dry whisk to combine. Put the sugar, coconut oil, lemon zest, lemon juice, and flaxseeds in the bowl of a stand mixer or a large bowl. Turn the stand mixer or a hand mixer to medium speed and beat until combined. Turn the mixer to low speed. Alternately add the flour mixture (in three additions) and the vegan buttermilk (in two additions), beginning and ending with the flour mixture, beating well after each addition. Turn off the mixer. Stir in the cider vinegar until just combined.

Spread the batter evenly in the prepared pans using a rubber spatula, smoothing the tops. Bake in the center of the oven for 18 to 22 minutes, until a toothpick inserted in the center of each cake comes out clean. The cakes will be golden brown, will begin to pull away from the sides of the pans, and will spring back when lightly touched.

Let cool in the pans for 10 minutes. Carefully remove the cakes from the pans and transfer them to a cooling rack. Let cool completely.

To make the filling, put the cranberries, apple, and agave nectar in a medium saucepan and bring to a boil over medium heat. Cook until the cranberries begin to pop, about 7 minutes. Decrease the heat to low and cook, stirring occasionally, for 10 to 15 minutes, until the apple is soft and the mixture is very thick. Remove from the heat. Stir in the vanilla extract and salt. Taste for sweetness, adding additional agave nectar if desired.

Per serving: 527 calories, 4 g protein, 31 g fat (18 g sat), 64 g carbohydrates, 259 mg sodium, 133 mg calcium, 6 g fiber

1 teaspoon vanilla extract

⅛ teaspoon fine sea salt

PECAN CRUMBLE *(can be prepared up to 1 day in advance)*

⅓ cup sorghum flour

⅓ cup teff flour

¼ cup unrefined cane sugar

2 tablespoons tapioca flour

½ teaspoon xanthan gum

½ teaspoon ground cinnamon

¼ teaspoon fine sea salt

2 tablespoons vegan buttery spread, softened

¼ cup nondairy milk

1 cup chopped pecans

LEMON SAUCE

¾ cup water

⅓ cup agave nectar

1½ teaspoons finely grated lemon zest

⅛ teaspoon fine sea salt

¼ cup freshly squeezed lemon juice

2 tablespoons tapioca flour

1 teaspoon vegan buttery spread

¼ teaspoon vanilla extract

FINISHING TOUCHES

About 2½ cups Whipped Topping (page 24; prepared and refrigerated until needed)

Scrape the filling into a medium bowl using a rubber spatula. Refrigerate until completely cool.

To make the crumble, preheat the oven to 300 degrees F. Line a baking sheet with parchment paper or a Silpat liner.

Put the sorghum flour, teff flour, sugar, tapioca flour, xanthan gum, cinnamon, and salt in the bowl of a stand mixer or large bowl and stir with a dry whisk to combine. Add the buttery spread. Using the stand mixer or a hand mixer, beat on medium-high speed until the buttery spread is mixed throughout the flour mixture. Add the nondairy milk and mix on low speed until the mixture starts to come together in small clusters. Turn off the mixer. Stir in the pecans. Using your fingers, crumble the mixture in a single layer onto the prepared baking sheet. Bake on the middle rack for 20 to 22 minutes, until the crumble begins to feel firm. Remove from the oven. Break up any large pieces with your fingers while the crumble is still warm. Let cool completely.

To make the lemon sauce, put the water, agave nectar, lemon zest, and salt in a small saucepan and whisk to combine. Cook over medium-high heat just until the mixture begins to bubble. Put the lemon juice and tapioca flour in a small bowl and whisk until no lumps remain. Add the tapioca flour mixture to the agave nectar mixture in the saucepan. Cook, whisking constantly, until the mixture thickens and coats the back of a spoon, about 1 minute. Pour the mixture into a small bowl and stir in the buttery spread and vanilla extract to complete the sauce. Refrigerate until cold, about 1 hour.

To assemble the trifle, cut the cakes into ¾-inch cubes. Put about one-third of the cake in a trifle bowl or large serving bowl, at least 3 quarts in volume. Drizzle with one-quarter of the lemon sauce. Spread one-third of the filling on top, followed by one-third of the Whipped Topping. Sprinkle with one-third of the crumble. Repeat the sequence twice in the same order: cake, lemon sauce, filling, Whipped Topping, and crumble. Drizzle with the remaining sauce.

Refrigerate for 6 hours before serving.

TIP: The cake, cranberry filling, and pecan crumble can all be made one day in advance, leaving only the lemon sauce to be made the day of assembly. Let the cakes cool completely, then wrap tightly in plastic wrap and store at room temperature. Cover and store the cranberry filling in the refrigerator. Put the pecan crumble in a container with a tight-fitting lid and store at room temperature.

Decadence—you've arrived. This dessert sandwiches layers of rich chocolate buttercream and fresh strawberries among oversized chocolate chip cookies. Time in the refrigerator lets flavors mingle, resulting in a luscious icebox cake that will satisfy, well, everyone.

CHOCOLATY Chocolate Chip Cookie ICEBOX CAKE

FREE OF: NUTS, PEANUTS, YEAST

YIELD: 10 SERVINGS

CHOCOLATE CHIP COOKIES *(can be prepared up to 1 day in advance)*

¾ cup vegan buttery spread

2 tablespoons ground flaxseeds

1 cup plus 2 tablespoons sorghum flour

½ cup teff flour

½ cup tapioca flour

1 teaspoon xanthan gum

¾ teaspoon baking soda

½ teaspoon fine sea salt

1 cup unrefined cane sugar

¼ cup unsweetened nondairy milk

2 teaspoons vanilla extract

⅔ cup nondairy semisweet chocolate chips

CHOCOLATE BUTTERCREAM

¾ cup puréed avocado flesh (about 1 large avocado)

¼ cup vegan buttery spread

¾ cup natural unsweetened cocoa powder, sifted

2 teaspoons vanilla extract

2 tablespoons unsweetened nondairy milk, plus more as needed

2⅔ cups confectioners' sugar, sifted

To make the cookies, position the oven rack in the middle of the oven. Preheat the oven to 325 degrees F. Line three 9-inch round pans with parchment paper.

Put the buttery spread in a medium saucepan and cook over medium heat until just melted. Remove from the heat and stir in the flaxseeds. Let stand until thickened, about 5 minutes. Put the sorghum flour, teff flour, tapioca flour, xanthan gum, baking soda, and salt in a medium bowl and stir with a dry whisk to combine. Put the flaxseed mixture, sugar, nondairy milk, and vanilla extract in the bowl of a stand mixer or a large bowl. Using the stand mixer or a hand mixer, beat on medium-high speed until well combined, about 2 minutes. Turn the mixer to low speed. Gradually add the flour mixture to the sugar mixture, beating until well combined. Turn off the mixer. Stir in the chocolate chips. Divide the dough into three equal portions. Put each portion into one of the lined baking pans and pat it into a disk about 8 inches in diameter.

Bake on the middle rack for 13 to 16 minutes, until the cookies are firm and just starting to crack around the edges. Let cool in the pans for 10 minutes. Carefully remove the cookies from the pans and transfer them to a cooling rack. Let cool completely.

To make the buttercream, put the avocado flesh and buttery spread in the bowl of a stand mixer or a large bowl. Using the stand mixer or a hand mixer, beat on medium-high speed until well combined and smooth.

Turn the mixer to low speed. Add the cocoa powder, vanilla extract, and 2 tablespoons of the nondairy milk and beat until well combined. Add 1 cup of the confectioners' sugar

Per serving: 607 calories, 7 g protein, 28 g fat (9 g sat), 89 g carbohydrates, 380 mg sodium, 52 mg calcium, 9 g fiber

FINISHING TOUCHES

2½ cups sliced strawberries, about ¼ inch thick

and beat until smooth. Alternately add the remaining confectioners' sugar and up to 1 tablespoon of additional nondairy milk as needed until the mixture is smooth. Turn the mixer to high speed and beat for 4 to 5 minutes to make a very creamy buttercream.

To assemble the icebox cake, put one of the cookies on a large plate. Spread a thick layer of the buttercream on top; the layer must be thick enough that you can push the strawberries into it. Gently press one-third of the strawberries into the thick layer of buttercream. Spread a thin layer of the buttercream on the bottom of the second cookie so it will stick on top of the strawberries. After putting the second cookie on top of the strawberries, repeat the sequence in the same order: cookie, thick layer of buttercream, and strawberries. Spread a thin layer of the buttercream on the bottom of the third cookie so it will stick on top of the strawberries. After putting the third cookie on top of the strawberries, top the cookie with a thick layer of buttercream and the remaining strawberries.

Refrigerate the icebox cake for 8 hours before serving (the cookies should be soft).

This icebox cake features spicy gingersnap cookies layered with a rich pumpkin cream. And like other icebox cakes, it's not only beautiful but also easy to prepare in advance, making it the perfect dessert for a holiday potluck.

GINGERSNAP-PUMPKIN Icebox Cake

FREE OF: PEANUTS, YEAST

YIELD: 10 SERVINGS

GINGERSNAP COOKIES *(can be prepared up to 2 days in advance)*

Scant ¾ cup unrefined cane sugar
⅔ cup coconut oil, melted
¼ cup molasses
2 tablespoons nondairy milk
1 tablespoon ground flaxseeds
1 cup sorghum flour
½ cup teff flour
½ cup tapioca flour
2½ teaspoons ground ginger
1¾ teaspoons baking soda
1½ teaspoons ground cinnamon
1 teaspoon xanthan gum
½ teaspoon ground cloves
¼ teaspoon fine sea salt

To make the cookies, position an oven rack in the lower third of the oven. Preheat the oven to 375 degrees F. Line two baking sheets with parchment paper.

Put the sugar, coconut oil, molasses, nondairy milk, and flaxseeds in the bowl of a stand mixer or a large bowl. Using the stand mixer or a hand mixer, beat on medium-high speed until well combined. Put the sorghum flour, teff flour, tapioca flour, ginger, baking soda, cinnamon, xanthan gum, cloves, and salt in a medium bowl and whisk until well combined. Turn the mixer to low speed. Gradually add the flour mixture to the sugar mixture, beating until well mixed. Turn off the mixer.

For each cookie, roll about 1 heaping tablespoon of dough into a ball between the palms of your hands. Put the ball on the lined baking sheet. Repeat with the remaining dough. There should be a total of 18 balls. Lightly flatten each ball with your palm.

Bake in the lower third of the oven for 10 to 12 minutes, just until the edges begin to firm. Let cool on the baking sheet for 5 minutes. Carefully remove the cookies from the baking sheet and transfer them to a cooling rack. Let cool completely. Once the cookies are cool, make the pumpkin cream.

Per serving: 530 calories, 6 g protein, 34 g fat (22 g sat), 53 g carbohydrates, 296 mg sodium, 5 mg calcium, 4 g fiber

PUMPKIN CREAM

1¼ cups mashed cooked or canned pumpkin

½ cup plus 2 tablespoons roasted creamy cashew butter

1 (14-ounce) can coconut milk, chilled

1 teaspoon finely grated lemon zest

3 tablespoons freshly squeezed lemon juice

½ teaspoon vanilla extract

¼ teaspoon plus ⅛ teaspoon fine sea salt

½ cup confectioners' sugar, sifted

1 tablespoon coconut oil, melted

To make the pumpkin cream, put the pumpkin, cashew butter, coconut milk, lemon zest, lemon juice, vanilla extract, and salt in a food processor and process for 5 minutes. Add the confectioners' sugar and process for 2 minutes. With the food processor running, add the coconut oil in a thin stream and process for 1 minute.

To assemble the icebox cake, put about six cookies in a 9-inch springform pan, breaking them if necessary to cover most of the pan's bottom (it's okay to leave small gaps). Spread one-third of the pumpkin cream on top of the cookies. Repeat the sequence twice in the same order, finishing with the pumpkin cream, to form the cake.

Put the cake in the freezer for 20 minutes, then transfer it to the refrigerator. Refrigerate the icebox cake for 18 hours before serving (the cookies should be soft).

Ice Cream and Frozen Desserts

I go running when I have to. When the ice-cream truck is doing sixty.

WENDY LEIBMAN, STAND-UP COMEDIENNE

See Classic Chocolate Ice Cream, page 124.

My favorite desserts generally revolve (and often evolve) around ice cream . . . I just can't get enough. That goes for classics, such as chocolate, strawberry, and vanilla, as well as fruit-inspired treats and sundaes of all sorts, including Hot Fudge Sundaes in Sugar Cone Bowls (page 132). The good news is that you don't have to forgo the ultimate frozen dessert just because you avoid dairy-based foods. Plus, these homemade goodies lack the saturated fat, preservatives, and unpronounceable additives that abound in commercial versions. And more good news: homemade ice cream can be made in an ice-cream maker or by hand, so you don't have to buy special equipment if you don't want to.

ICE CREAM INSIGHTS

Fresh, simple, and oh-so-creamy homemade ice cream has a texture and flavor that surpassess anything that can be found in the grocer's freezer. For a rich and delicious dessert, I like to start all varieties of ice cream with the same combination of ingredients:

Coconut milk and coconut beverage. Full-fat coconut milk, which is sold in cans, is about 17 percent fat, and coconut milk beverage, which is sold in cartons, is about 8 percent fat; when paired, these two ingredients make for a creamy, rich ice-cream base. This coconutty combo stands in for the mixture of heavy cream (about 38 percent fat) and whole milk (about 4 percent fat) used in conventional ice-cream recipes. The coconut products, which are considerably lower in fat, produce a similar and satisfying texture. If you can't find coconut milk beverage, almond milk and soy milk are suitable alternatives; however, both are lower in fat and produce a less creamy result.

Tapioca flour. In eggless ice cream, tapioca flour acts as a thickener and creates a custard that adds a creamy texture. Tapioca flour also absorbs excess water, eliminating iciness.

Raw macadamia butter. Raw macadamia butter is high in fat, velvety in texture, and neutral in flavor, and all of these characteristics add depth and richness to homemade ice cream. If the macadamia butter isn't completely smooth, pour the ice-cream base through a fine-mesh strainer when transferring it to a bowl to cool. Though macadamia butter is preferred, you can use other raw nut butters that have neutral flavors, such as cashew or sunflower seed butter (see page 16 for making your own nut butter).

Using an Ice-Cream Maker

Here are some basic tips for making ice cream in an ice-cream maker:

- Read the manufacturer's instructions before starting.
- Store the ice-cream maker canister in the freezer for 48 hours before churning; if you have one, use a deep freezer.
- Refrigerate the ice-cream base for 8 hours before churning.
- Sometimes a thin layer of solid ice cream can coat the canister after churning. To avoid this, pour the ice-cream base into the canister after starting the machine, instead of filling it first and then turning the power on.
- Fill the canister only about three-quarters full, which will give the mixture enough room to aerate.
- Right out of the freezer, homemade ice cream is firmer than store-bought versions. Let it stand at room temperature for about 20 minutes before scooping.
- Flavors intensify and meld both as the ice-cream base cools and after churning. If you choose to tweak the amounts of sweetener, extracts, or spices, do so just before churning.
- If you're adding ingredients such as chocolate chips or nuts, add them in the last minute of churning or mix them in by hand after churning.

Making Ice Cream by Hand

Although it's convenient to use an ice-cream maker, you don't need a machine to make ice cream at home. Ice cream made with a machine is typically smoother and creamier than handmade ice cream, however, which might tempt you to make the investment.

The key to making ice cream by hand is to take steps to prevent ice crystals from forming. This requires that you're at home and available to break up the ice crystals as they form. So set aside an afternoon to give it a try. Here's how:

- After combining the ingredients, pour the mixture into a baking dish and let it cool in the refrigerator.
- Once it's chilled, put the mixture in the freezer for 45 minutes.
- During that time, the mixture will start to freeze around the edges. Stir the mixture vigorously with a whisk or firm spatula, breaking up the frozen pieces. Alternatively, use a hand mixer or immersion blender.
- Put the mixture back in the freezer and continue checking it every 30 minutes, stirring vigorously to break up the crystals.

- Continue this process, which takes about 4 hours, until the ice cream is the consistency of soft-serve.
- Serve immediately if a soft consistency is desired; for firmer ice cream, see the storing instructions (below).

Storing Ice Cream

Whether churned in a machine or made by hand, homemade ice cream is the consistency of soft-serve. To create a firmer and perfectly scoopable texture, transfer the ice cream to a shallow, flat container and put it in the freezer for about 3 hours. To prevent ice crystals from forming, cover the surface with a layer of plastic wrap before covering the container with a lid. If the ice cream is very hard, let it sit at room temperature for about 20 minutes before scooping. Homemade ice cream is best when eaten within 4 days—but really, is it going to last that long?

This classic ice-cream flavor features not-so-classic ingredients. Use this recipe as a base for your own ice-cream experiments. Three variations follow the recipe to give you options and inspiration.

VERY VANILLA Ice Cream

FREE OF: CORN, PEANUTS, SEEDS, YEAST

YIELD: APPROXIMATELY 1½ QUARTS

1½ cups unsweetened coconut milk beverage

1 (14-ounce) **can full-fat coconut milk**

⅔ cup agave nectar

¼ teaspoon fine sea salt

3 tablespoons tapioca flour

2 tablespoons raw macadamia butter (see sidebar, page 16)

2 teaspoons vanilla extract

Put 1¼ cups of the coconut milk beverage and the canned coconut milk, agave nectar, and salt in a medium saucepan and whisk to combine. Cook over medium-high heat just until the mixture begins to bubble. Put the remaining ¼ cup of coconut milk beverage and the tapioca flour in a small bowl and whisk until no lumps remain. Add the tapioca flour mixture to the mixture in the saucepan, whisking constantly. Cook over medium heat, stirring occasionally, until the mixture thickens and coats the back of a spoon, about 3 minutes. Remove from the heat.

Put the macadamia butter in a small bowl. Using a ladle, transfer about ¼ cup of the thickened mixture to the bowl and whisk until smooth. Pour the macadamia butter mixture into the saucepan and add the vanilla extract. Whisk until the mixture is smooth; this will be the ice-cream base. Scrape the ice-cream base into a large bowl using a rubber spatula. Let it cool completely at room temperature, then refrigerate for 8 hours.

If you're using an ice-cream maker, follow the manufacturer's instructions. If you're making the ice cream by hand, see page 120. Serve immediately for soft-serve ice cream or freeze.

Vanilla Bean Ice Cream: Omit the vanilla extract. Scrape the seeds of one vanilla bean into the coconut milk mixture before adding the tapioca flour. Cook over medium-high heat, stirring occasionally, just until the mixture bubbles, then stir in the pod and its contents. Remove from the heat, cover, and let stand for 1 hour. Remove the pod, squeezing out any flavorful liquid. Cook over medium heat, stirring occasionally, until the mixture thickens and coats the back of a spoon, about 3 minutes. Remove from the heat and proceed as directed.

Per ½ cup: 150 calories, 1 g protein, 9 g fat (6 g sat), 19 g carbohydrates, 11 mg sodium, 2 mg calcium, 0 g fiber

Maple Ice Cream: Replace the agave nectar with ¾ cup of pure maple syrup. Omit the vanilla extract. If the maple syrup flavor isn't strong, add 1 teaspoon of maple extract to the coconut milk mixture. Proceed as directed.

Gingerbread Ice Cream: Decrease the agave nectar to ¼ cup and add 3 tablespoons of molasses, 2½ teaspoons of ground ginger, 1 teaspoon of ground cinnamon, ½ teaspoon of ground nutmeg, and ¼ teaspoon of cloves to the coconut milk mixture. Proceed as directed.

Pure and simple, creamy chocolate ice cream makes me go weak in the knees. For a real treat, use this ice cream in the Hot Fudge Sundaes in Sugar Cone Bowls (page 132), then top with fresh raspberries and cacao nibs.

Classic CHOCOLATE ICE CREAM

FREE OF: CORN, NUTS, PEANUTS, SEEDS, YEAST

YIELD: APPROXIMATELY 1½ QUARTS

- **1½ cups unsweetened coconut milk beverage**
- **1** (14-ounce) **can full-fat coconut milk**
- **½ cup agave nectar**
- **6 tablespoons natural unsweetened cocoa powder, sifted**
- **½ teaspoon fine sea salt**
- **2 tablespoons tapioca flour**
- **½ cup nondairy semisweet chocolate chips**
- **1 tablespoon vanilla extract**

Put 1¼ cups of the coconut milk beverage and the canned coconut milk, agave nectar, cocoa powder, and salt in a medium saucepan and whisk until no lumps remain. Cook over medium-high heat just until the mixture begins to bubble. Put the remaining ¼ cup of coconut milk beverage and the tapioca flour in a small bowl and whisk until no lumps remain. Add the tapioca flour mixture to the mixture in the saucepan, whisking constantly. Cook over medium heat, stirring occasionally, until the mixture thickens and coats the back of a spoon, about 3 minutes. Decrease the heat to low. Add the chocolate chips and continue to cook, whisking occasionally, until they are melted, about 2 minutes. Remove from the heat. Stir in the vanilla extract until well combined; this will be the ice-cream base. Scrape the ice-cream base into a large bowl using a rubber spatula. Let it cool completely at room temperature, then refrigerate for 8 hours.

If you're using an ice-cream maker, follow the manufacturer's instructions. If you're making the ice cream by hand, see page 120. Serve immediately for soft-serve ice cream or freeze.

Mexican Dark Chocolate Ice Cream: Replace the cocoa powder with unsweetened dark cocoa powder. Add 1½ teaspoons of ground cinnamon and ⅛ teaspoon plus a pinch of ground cayenne to the coconut milk mixture. Increase the vanilla extract to 1½ teaspoons. Proceed as directed.

Per ½ cup: 176 calories, 2 g protein, 10 g fat (7 g sat), 20 g carbohydrates, 105 mg sodium, 0 mg calcium, 2 g fiber

Here's an ice cream with a grown-up flavor that kids will enjoy too. Citrus lovers will adore its refreshing balance of tartness, sweetness, and slight bitterness. Be sure to zest the grapefruit before peeling it.

Grapefruit ICE CREAM

FREE OF: CORN, PEANUTS, SEEDS, YEAST

YIELD: APPROXIMATELY 1½ QUARTS

- **2 teaspoons finely grated red grapefruit zest**
- **1 red grapefruit, peeled**
- **⅔ cup agave nectar**
- **1¼ cups unsweetened coconut milk beverage**
- **1** (14-ounce) **can full-fat coconut milk**
- **¼ teaspoon fine sea salt**
- **3 tablespoons tapioca flour**
- **2 tablespoons raw macadamia butter** (see sidebar, page 16)
- **2 teaspoons vanilla extract**

Put the grapefruit zest and the peeled grapefruit in a food processor and process until smooth. Pour the mixture into a medium saucepan. Stir in the agave nectar until well combined. Cook over medium heat, stirring occasionally, until the mixture has reduced to 1 cup, about 25 minutes. (The mixture should be similar in consistency to maple syrup.) Pour the mixture into a large bowl.

Put 1 cup of the coconut milk beverage and the canned coconut milk and salt in the saucepan and whisk to combine. Cook over medium-high heat just until the mixture begins to bubble. Return the grapefruit mixture to the saucepan and stir until well combined.

Put the remaining ¼ cup of coconut milk beverage and the tapioca flour in a small bowl and whisk until no lumps remain. Add the tapioca flour mixture to the mixture in the saucepan, whisking constantly. Cook over medium heat, stirring occasionally, until the mixture thickens and coats the back of a spoon, about 3 minutes. Remove from the heat.

Put the macadamia butter in a small bowl. Using a ladle, transfer about ¼ cup of the thickened mixture to the bowl and whisk until smooth. Pour the macadamia butter mixture into the saucepan and add the vanilla extract. Whisk until the mixture is smooth; this will be the ice-cream base. Scrape the ice-cream base into a large bowl using a rubber spatula. Let it cool completely at room temperature, then refrigerate for 8 hours.

If you're using an ice-cream maker, follow the manufacturer's instructions. If you're making the ice cream by hand, see page 120. Serve immediately for soft-serve ice cream or freeze.

Clementine Spice Ice Cream: Replace the grapefruit zest with clementine zest and the grapefruit with 5 peeled clementines. Decrease the agave nectar to ½ cup and add ½ teaspoon of ground ginger, ½ teaspoon of ground cinnamon, ½ teaspoon of ground nutmeg, and ½ teaspoon of cloves to the coconut milk mixture. Proceed as directed.

Per ½ cup: 154 calories, 1 g protein, 9 g fat (6 g sat), 20 g carbohydrates, 10 mg sodium, 15 mg calcium, 1 g fiber

Silky, rich, and oh-so-nutty, this ice cream is easy to make and becomes even more flavorful with time. The brownie bites add texture and bursts of chocolaty goodness. This recipe makes enough brownie bites for two batches of ice cream, so store the leftover brownie bites in a resealable plastic bag in the freezer and use them within three months.

PEANUT BUTTER-BROWNIE BITE Ice Cream

FREE OF: CORN, GRAINS, SEEDS, YEAST

YIELD: APPROXIMATELY 1½ QUARTS

BROWNIE BITES *(can be prepared up to 2 days in advance)*

1 cup almonds

5 tablespoons natural unsweetened cocoa powder, preferably dark

¼ teaspoon plus ⅛ teaspoon fine sea salt

¾ cup pitted soft honey dates (see page 14)

1 teaspoon vanilla extract

PEANUT BUTTER ICE CREAM

1½ cups unsweetened coconut milk beverage

1 (14-ounce) **can full-fat coconut milk**

¾ cup creamy natural peanut butter (see tips)

½ cup agave nectar

2 teaspoons vanilla extract

¼ teaspoon fine sea salt (see tips)

To make the brownie bites, put the almonds, cocoa powder, and salt in a food processor and process until the almonds are coarsely chopped, about 45 seconds. Add the dates and vanilla extract and process until the mixture begins to stick together, about 2 minutes. To test, squeeze a bit of the mixture in your hand. If it doesn't stick together, pulse the mixture a few more times.

Using a rubber spatula, scrape the mixture onto a piece of waxed paper and knead until the mixture fully comes together and forms a dough. Top with a second piece of waxed paper and roll out the dough using a rolling pin, forming a ¼-inch-thick slab (it doesn't have to be a perfect rectangle). Put in the freezer until very firm, about 20 minutes. Once the slab is very firm, slice it into ¼- to ½-inch cubes using a sharp knife. Transfer the brownie bites to a freezer-safe container and put in the freezer until the ice cream is ready.

To make the ice cream, put the coconut milk beverage, canned coconut milk, peanut butter, agave nectar, vanilla extract, and salt in a food processor and process until well combined; this will be the ice-cream base. Pour the ice-cream base into a large bowl, then refrigerate for 8 hours.

If you're using an ice-cream maker, follow the manufacturer's instructions. If you're making the ice cream by hand, see page 120.

Scrape the ice cream into a large freezer-safe container using a rubber spatula. Remove the brownie bites from the freezer. Stir 1½ cups of the brownie bites into the ice cream and return the unused portion to the freezer for later. Serve immediately for soft-serve ice cream or freeze.

Peanut Butter Ice Cream: Omit the brownie bites.

Per ½ cup: 250 calories, 6 g protein, 17 g fat (7 g sat), 20 g carbohydrates, 105 mg sodium, 18 mg calcium, 2 g fiber

Almond Butter–Brownie Bite Ice Cream: Use creamy roasted almond butter instead of peanut butter.

TIPS

- If the peanut butter is slightly grainy and you would prefer a smoother texture, pour the ice-cream base through a fine-mesh strainer before refrigerating it.
- The amount of salt in the peanut butter will influence the amount of salt you need to add to the ice-cream mixture. After adding the salt, taste the ice-cream mixture. If the flavor seems a bit dull, add an extra ¼ teaspoon of salt to the mixture and stir until well combined.

Roasted strawberries bring incomparable richness to this **sweet and fruity** ice cream, which pairs up perfectly with **brownie-like cookies** to form unforgettable sandwiches. The cookies and ice-cream base can both be made one day in advance, making assembly a breeze the next day. To make this ice cream by hand, see the tip (page 120).

STRAWBERRY ICE-CREAM Sandwiches

FREE OF: YEAST

YIELD: 12 SANDWICHES, DEPENDING ON SIZE

ROASTED STRAWBERRY ICE CREAM

2 cups sliced fresh strawberries, about ¼ inch thick

2 tablespoons unrefined cane sugar

1 tablespoon freshly squeezed lemon juice

1 (14-ounce) **can full-fat coconut milk**

¾ cup unsweetened coconut milk beverage

⅓ cup agave nectar

¼ teaspoon fine sea salt

3 tablespoons tapioca flour

2 tablespoons raw macadamia butter (see sidebar, page 16)

½ teaspoon vanilla extract

BROWNIE COOKIES *(can be prepared up to 2 days in advance)*

6 tablespoons strong brewed coffee, warm

2 tablespoons ground flaxseeds

¾ cup natural unsweetened cocoa powder, sifted

½ cup sorghum flour

¼ cup teff flour

¼ cup arrowroot starch

1 teaspoon xanthan gum

1 teaspoon baking powder

To make the ice cream, preheat the oven to 375 degrees F. Line a baking sheet with parchment paper or a Silpat liner. Put the strawberries, sugar, and lemon juice in a medium bowl and stir to combine. Arrange the strawberries on the prepared baking sheet in a single layer. Bake for about 15 minutes, until the strawberries are soft and juicy. Using a slotted spoon to avoid the fruit juices, transfer the strawberries to a cutting board. Finely chop the strawberries using a sharp knife.

Put the canned coconut milk, ½ cup of the coconut milk beverage, the agave nectar, and salt in a medium saucepan and whisk to combine. Cook over medium-high heat just until the mixture begins to bubble. Put the remaining ¼ cup of coconut milk beverage and the tapioca flour in a small bowl and whisk until no lumps remain. Add the tapioca flour mixture to the mixture in the saucepan, whisking constantly. Cook over medium heat, stirring occasionally, until the mixture thickens and coats the back of a spoon, about 3 minutes. Remove from the heat.

Put the macadamia butter in a small bowl. Using a ladle, transfer about ¼ cup of the thickened mixture to the bowl and whisk until smooth. Pour the macadamia butter mixture into the saucepan and add the vanilla extract. Whisk until the mixture is smooth; this will be the ice-cream base. Scrape the ice-cream base into a large bowl using a rubber spatula. Let it cool completely at room temperature, then refrigerate for 8 hours.

To make the cookies, put the coffee and flaxseeds in a small bowl and stir to combine. Let stand until thickened, about 5 minutes.

Put the cocoa powder, sorghum flour, teff flour, arrowroot starch, xanthan gum, baking powder, and salt in a medium

Per sandwich: 277 calories, 3 g protein, 14 g fat (7 g sat), 40 g carbohydrates, 140 mg sodium, 27 mg calcium, 4 g fiber

¼ teaspoon fine sea salt

1 scant cup unrefined cane sugar

¼ cup vegan buttery spread, at room temperature

1½ teaspoons vanilla extract

bowl and stir with a dry whisk to combine. Put the sugar and buttery spread in the bowl of a stand mixer or a large bowl. Using the stand mixer or a hand mixer, beat on medium-high speed until smooth and fluffy, about 2 minutes. Add the flaxseed mixture and vanilla extract and beat until well combined. Turn the mixer to low speed. Gradually add the flour mixture to the sugar mixture, mixing until well combined to form a sticky dough.

Put a large piece of plastic wrap on a flat surface. Scrape the dough onto the plastic wrap using a rubber spatula. Wrap the dough tightly in the plastic wrap and shape it into a disk. Refrigerate for 30 minutes.

Position an oven rack in the middle of the oven. Preheat the oven to 350 degrees F. Remove the dough from the refrigerator. Unwrap the dough and divide it into two equal pieces. Rewrap one of the pieces and return it to the refrigerator. Put the other piece of dough on a piece of parchment paper measuring at least 11 x 10 inches. Roll out the dough using a rolling pin, forming a rectangle about 9 x 8 inches. (If the dough is very sticky, keep it covered with the plastic wrap while rolling.) Transfer the parchment paper with the rolled dough to a baking sheet. Bake on the middle rack for 10 to 12 minutes, until the top is dry to the touch. Repeat with the second piece of dough. Let both cool completely.

When you're ready to assemble the sandwiches, freeze the ice cream according to the ice-cream maker manufacturer's instructions. If you're making the ice cream by hand, see page 120 and the tip on page 130.

To assemble the sandwiches, line a 13 x 9-inch metal pan with aluminum foil, leaving a few inches of foil hanging over the sides of the pan. Invert one of the cooled cookies onto the aluminum foil, so the bottom is facing up. Top with the freshly churned ice cream, spreading it evenly using a rubber spatula but leaving about 2 inches from the edges so it doesn't seep out the sides. Invert the second cookie onto a cutting board, so the bottom is facing up. Invert the cookie onto the ice cream so the bottom is now facing the ice cream. Use the aluminum foil to cover as much of the ice-cream sandwich as possible. Top with another piece of foil to completely cover the top and sides of the sandwich. Gently press down on the sandwich with your hands, using just enough pressure so the ice-cream filling spreads to the edges and is evenly distributed; you'll need to peek under the foil to check. Wrap the sandwich securely with the foil and put it in the freezer for 8 hours.

Remove the sandwich from the freezer and lift it out of the pan. Put it on a cutting board and let it stand at room temperature for 10 minutes. Cut it into twelve small sandwiches using a sharp knife. Let the sandwiches stand for 10 minutes before serving. If not serving immediately, individually wrap each sandwich with aluminum foil and store in the freezer. When serving directly from the freezer, let stand for about 20 minutes at room temperature.

TIP: If you're making the ice cream by hand, make the cookies in between stirring the ice cream. The cookies will be baked and cooled by the time the ice cream is at the soft-serve stage and ready for assembly.

Mint and chocolate make a winning combination, and this frozen treat features a hardened swirl of chocolate that you'll want to chase with your spoon. This ice cream relies on the freshest ingredients, so keep that in mind when choosing the mint leaves and avocados.

Mint-Chocolate SWIRL ICE CREAM

FREE OF: CORN, GRAINS, NUTS, PEANUTS, SEEDS, YEAST

YIELD: APPROXIMATELY 1½ QUARTS

MINT ICE CREAM

1 (14-ounce) **can full-fat coconut milk**

¾ cup unsweetened coconut milk beverage

45 fresh mint leaves, stemmed

Pinch fine sea salt

1½ cups mashed avocado flesh (about 3 small avocados)

½ cup agave nectar

1 to 3 teaspoons peppermint extract (optional)

CHOCOLATE STRACCIATELLA

½ cup nondairy semisweet chocolate chips

1 teaspoon coconut oil

Per ½ cup: 192 calories, 2 g protein, 13 g fat (7 g sat), 20 g carbohydrates, 9 mg sodium, 10 mg calcium, 3 g fiber

To make the ice cream, put the canned coconut milk, coconut milk beverage, mint leaves, and salt in a medium saucepan and cook over medium heat until steaming. Remove from the heat, cover, and let come to room temperature. Transfer to a storage container and refrigerate for 8 hours.

Pour the coconut milk mixture through a fine-mesh strainer into a food processor, pressing down firmly on the strainer contents to extract as much mint flavor as possible, then discard the strainer contents. Put the avocado flesh and agave nectar in the food processor with the coconut milk mixture and process until smooth; this will be the ice-cream base. Taste and stir in the peppermint extract, 1 teaspoon at a time, if a stronger flavor is desired. (Depending on the potency of the mint leaves, you may not need any peppermint extract.) Scrape the ice-cream base into a large bowl using a rubber spatula, then refrigerate for 1 hour.

If you're using an ice-cream maker, follow the manufacturer's instructions. If you're making the ice cream by hand, see page 120.

To make the chocolate stracciatella, melt the chocolate chips and coconut oil using the microwave or stove-top method (see page 20). Scrape the chocolate mixture into a glass measuring cup using a rubber spatula.

If you're using an ice-cream maker, when the ice cream has finished churning, carefully pour the chocolate mixture in a slow stream directly into the canister, continuing to churn for 30 seconds. If you're making the ice cream by hand, drizzle the chocolate onto the ice cream when it has a soft-serve consistency. Stir, then drizzle some more chocolate, stirring and repeating until all the chocolate is used. The chocolate will harden in streaks.

Serve immediately for soft-serve ice cream or freeze.

When I was a kid and we'd go out for ice cream, getting a sugar cone (over the plain variety) was such a treat. Now I know how easy it is to make sugar cones, and it's even easier to make sugar cone bowls. These sweet, edible bowls are a must for this unbeatable hot fudge sundae.

Hot Fudge Sundaes IN SUGAR CONE BOWLS

FREE OF: NUTS, PEANUTS, SEEDS, YEAST

YIELD: 12 SERVINGS, DEPENDING ON SIZE; ABOUT ¾ CUP HOT FUDGE SAUCE

SUGAR CONE BOWLS *(can be prepared up to 2 days in advance)*

1 cup sorghum flour

⅓ cup tapioca flour

¼ cup quinoa flour

1 teaspoon xanthan gum

1 cup full-fat canned coconut milk

1 tablespoon vanilla extract

1½ cups confectioners' sugar

½ teaspoon ground cinnamon

¼ teaspoon ground nutmeg

⅛ teaspoon fine sea salt

To make the bowls, put the sorghum flour, tapioca flour, quinoa flour, and xanthan gum in a medium bowl and stir with a dry whisk to combine. Put the canned coconut milk and vanilla extract in a large bowl and whisk until frothy. Sift the confectioners' sugar into the coconut milk mixture and stir until well combined. Stir in the flour mixture, cinnamon, nutmeg, and salt to make a smooth, thick batter. Let stand at room temperature for 30 minutes.

After the 30 minutes, position an oven rack in the middle of the oven. Preheat the oven to 375 degrees F. Line a baking sheet with parchment paper or a Silpat liner.

Scoop 2 rounded tablespoonfuls of the batter onto one half of the prepared baking sheet. Using a metal offset spatula, spread the batter into a thin disk, about 6½ inches in diameter and ⅛ inch thick. Make sure the batter is even in thickness (which is more important than the diameter). Repeat, forming another thin disk on the other half of the baking sheet.

Bake on the middle rack for 8 to 10 minutes, until the tops are dry and the edges are firm and start to turn golden. Remove the baking sheet from the oven and carefully flip each disk. Bake for 3 to 8 minutes longer, until golden all over and starting to brown on the edges.

Have two bowls, about 5 inches in diameter and 2 inches deep, ready to use as molds. Remove the baking sheet from the oven and, being careful not to burn your fingers but working quickly, maneuver a disk into one of the molds, forming it into a bowl shape. Repeat with the second disk. You'll need to move

Per bowl: 157 calories, 2 g protein, 4 g fat (3 g sat), 29 g carbohydrates, 5 mg sodium, 1 mg calcium, 1 g fiber

Per 2 tablespoons hot fudge: 151 calories, 2 g protein, 7 g fat (4 g sat), 23 g carbohydrates, 107 mg sodium, 17 mg calcium, 3 g fiber

Note: Analysis doesn't include nondairy ice cream for serving.

HOT FUDGE SAUCE

½ cup nondairy semisweet chocolate chips

¼ cup pure maple syrup

¼ cup nondairy milk

¼ cup unsweetened dark cocoa powder

¼ teaspoon fine sea salt

FOR SERVING

Nondairy ice cream (½ cup per serving)

swiftly because the disks start to firm once they are out of the oven. The first two bowls may not turn out perfectly but will serve as practice.

Continue making two bowls at a time until all the batter has been used. The baking sheet can remain hot between batches, which means subsequent batches may bake a little faster than the first batch, so check them a few minutes early. While a new batch is in the oven, remove the firm bowls from the molds. The bowls should be very crispy, similar to a sugar cone. If any of the bowls are too soft, simply put them back in the oven for about 45 seconds. They will soften and lose shape. When they turn golden, remove them from the oven and reform as directed.

To make the hot fudge, put the chocolate chips, maple syrup, nondairy milk, cocoa powder, and salt in a small saucepan. Cook over low heat, stirring occasionally, until the chocolate chips are melted. Whisk until smooth. Increase the heat to high and bring to a boil. Boil for 1 minute. Remove from the heat. Let cool for about 10 minutes before serving.

To serve, put the sugar cone bowls on small plates and scoop the ice cream into the bowls. Drizzle with the hot fudge sauce.

Store leftover bowls in a sealed container at room temperature for up to 5 days. Store leftover hot fudge sauce in a sealed jar in the refrigerator and reheat before using.

Featuring spiced apples, pears, and dried fruits, this sundae will steer you right in the wintertime. The fruit mixture is served warm with maple-spiced nuts and vanilla ice cream. If you have any leftover fruit, warm it and use it as a pancake topping.

SLOW-BAKED Winter Fruit Sundaes WITH CANDIED NUTS

FREE OF: CORN, LEGUMES, PEANUTS, SEEDS, YEAST

YIELD: 8 SERVINGS

SLOW-BAKED WINTER FRUIT

1 large orange

3 cups apple cider

¾ cup halved unsulfured dried calimyrna figs, packed

¾ cup unsulfured dried apricots, packed

½ cup unsulfured prunes, packed

3 tablespoons finely chopped candied ginger

¼ teaspoon ground cinnamon

⅛ teaspoon fine sea salt

2 large tart apples (see page 17), **unpeeled**

2 large pears (see page 18), **unpeeled**

MAPLE-CANDIED NUTS *(can be prepared up to 3 days in advance)*

1¾ cups unsalted raw nuts (see tip)

¾ teaspoon fine sea salt

¾ teaspoon ground cinnamon

¼ teaspoon ground nutmeg

¼ teaspoon ground cardamom

¼ teaspoon ground ginger

3 tablespoons pure maple syrup

To make the fruit, use a paring knife to cut the peel from the orange, removing the white pith. Slice the orange into ½-inch pieces, then cut each slice in half. Put the orange in a large bowl. Add the apple cider, figs, apricots, prunes, candied ginger, cinnamon, and salt and stir to combine. Cover with aluminum foil and let stand at room temperature for about 4 hours.

To make the nuts, position an oven rack on the lowest level of the oven. Preheat the oven to 350 degrees F. Line a baking sheet with parchment paper.

Put the nuts, salt, cinnamon, nutmeg, cardamom, and ginger in a medium bowl and stir until well combined. Put the maple syrup in a small saucepan and bring to a boil over high heat. Boil for 1 minute. Remove from the heat and pour over the nut mixture. Stir until the nut mixture is coated with the maple syrup. Spread the mixture onto the prepared baking sheet in a single layer. Bake on the lowest rack for 8 minutes, then stir and continue baking for 7 to 12 minutes, until fragrant and toasted. (The nuts will still feel wet to the touch.) Let cool completely on the pan. Break the mixture apart and store in a sealed container until needed.

After the fruit mixture has soaked, position the oven rack in the middle of the oven. Preheat the oven to 350 degrees F. Slice each apple and pear into about 10 wedges, then cut each wedge in half. Add the apples and pears to the dried fruit mixture and stir until well combined. Pour the fruit mixture into a shallow 3-quart baking dish and cover with aluminum foil. Bake on the middle rack for 30 to 40 minutes, until the liquid is bubbling and the pears and apples are soft. Remove the foil and let stand for about 25 minutes before serving.

Per serving: 402 calories, 7 g protein, 16 g fat (2 g sat), 64 g carbohydrates, 13 mg sodium, 112 mg calcium, 9 g fiber

Note: Analysis doesn't include Vanilla Bean Ice Cream for serving.

FOR SERVING

Vanilla Bean Ice Cream (page 122; ½ cup per serving)

To serve, use a ladle to transfer some of the fruit mixture into a bowl. Top with ½ cup of ice cream and sprinkle with some of the nuts. Leftover nuts can be stored in a sealed container in the freezer for up to 3 months.

TIP: Though you can use any combination of raw nuts, I love to use almonds, pecans, and walnuts to make this sweet, crunchy topping.

Together, all the components of this sundae are magical, although the brownies alone can put you under their spell. The soft-serve ice cream can be made in mere minutes, and the chocolate topping hardens as if by, well, magic.

MAGICAL Caramel-Swirled BROWNIE SUNDAES

FREE OF: PEANUTS, YEAST

YIELD: 9 SERVINGS

BROWNIE BATTER

6 tablespoons brewed coffee

2 tablespoons ground flaxseeds

6 tablespoons vegan buttery spread

2 tablespoons roasted creamy cashew butter

1 cup unrefined cane sugar

½ cup sorghum flour

¼ cup tapioca flour

½ teaspoon baking powder

¼ teaspoon xanthan gum

½ cup plus 2 tablespoons natural unsweetened cocoa powder

2 teaspoons vanilla extract

⅛ teaspoon fine sea salt

½ cup nondairy semisweet chocolate chips

CARAMEL SWIRL

7 tablespoons roasted creamy cashew butter

1 tablespoon vegan buttery spread

2 tablespoons pure maple syrup

1½ tablespoons agave nectar

½ teaspoon blackstrap molasses

1 teaspoon vanilla extract

½ teaspoon fine sea salt, plus more if desired

2 teaspoons tapioca flour

To make the brownies, position an oven rack in the middle of the oven. Preheat the oven to 325 degrees F. Line an 8-inch square baking pan with parchment paper.

Put the coffee and flaxseeds in the bowl of a stand mixer or a large bowl and stir to combine. Let stand until thickened, about 5 minutes. Put the buttery spread and cashew butter in a small saucepan and cook over medium heat, stirring occasionally, until melted. Stir in the sugar until well combined. Put the sorghum flour, tapioca flour, baking powder, and xanthan gum in a medium bowl and stir with a dry whisk to combine.

Add the sugar mixture to the flaxseed mixture. Using the stand mixer or a hand mixer, beat on low speed until well combined. Turn off the mixer. Add the cocoa powder, vanilla extract, and salt and beat on medium speed until well combined. Turn the mixer to low speed. Gradually add the flour mixture, stopping occasionally to scrape down the bowl if necessary, and beat until well combined to make a thick batter. Stir in the chocolate chips until well distributed. Spread the batter in the prepared pan using a rubber spatula, smoothing the top.

To make the caramel swirl, put the cashew butter, buttery spread, maple syrup, agave nectar, and blackstrap molasses in a saucepan and cook over low heat, stirring occasionally, until smooth and thick, about 5 minutes. Remove from the heat. Stir in the vanilla extract and ½ teaspoon of salt until well combined. Taste and stir in additional salt if desired (I prefer an additional ⅛ teaspoon). Stir in the tapioca flour until well combined. Drop spoonfuls of the caramel mixture on top of the brownie batter. Swirl the mixture into the batter using a butter knife. Smooth the top evenly with a rubber spatula. Bake on the

Per serving: 828 calories, 11 g protein, 47 g fat (23 g sat), 102 g carbohydrates, 82 mg sodium, 21 mg calcium, 10 g fiber

MAGICAL TOPPING

1 cup nondairy semisweet chocolate chips

¼ cup coconut oil

⅛ teaspoon fine sea salt

BANANA SOFT-SERVE *(start preparation 12 hours in advance)*

7 large bananas, peeled, cut into chunks, and frozen

2 tablespoons unsweetened nondairy milk

1 teaspoon vanilla extract

middle rack for 32 to 40 minutes, until a toothpick inserted in the center comes out moist but with no gooey bits attached to it. The sides will be firm and begin to pull away from the pan. Let cool completely in the pan.

To make the topping, melt the chocolate chips with the coconut oil and salt using the microwave or stove-top method (see page 20). Stir until well combined. Let stand until ready to assemble the dessert. Prepare the soft serve right before assembling and serving the dessert.

To make the soft-serve, remove the bananas from the freezer and put them in a food processor with the nondairy milk and vanilla extract. Process for about 5 minutes, until the mixture is smooth and creamy, stopping occasionally to scrape down the work bowl if necessary. (If your food processor is small, you may need to make the soft-serve in two batches.)

To assemble the sundaes, cut the brownies into 9 squares and put each one in a dish. Top each brownie with 1 scoop of the soft-serve. Spoon the topping over the soft-serve, covering each scoop completely. Let stand until the topping is firm, about 1 minute. Serve immediately. See the tip for making individual servings.

TIP: If you're not serving a crowd, store leftover brownies in a freezer-safe container in the freezer for up to 3 months and the chocolate topping in a sealed container at room temperature for up to 1 week. As long as you have frozen bananas in the freezer, you can make the soft-serve as needed. Process 1 small banana, about 1 teaspoon of nondairy milk, and a dash of vanilla extract per serving.

The classic frozen Mississippi Mud Pie gets a makeover with Kahlua-Coffee Ice Cream. Once you add the chocolate ganache, chocolate cookie-crumb crust, and roasted almonds, you'll have an irresistible and sophisticated dessert to serve your friends. The crust can be prepared one day in advance to make assembly quick and easy (see tips, page 140).

Frozen Kahlua MUD PIE

FREE OF: PEANUTS, SEEDS, YEAST

YIELD: 10 SLICES

KAHLUA-COFFEE ICE CREAM

1¼ cups unsweetened coconut milk beverage

1 (14-ounce) **can full-fat coconut milk**

½ cup agave nectar

3 single-serve packets extra-bold instant coffee (see tips, page 140)

¼ teaspoon plus ⅛ teaspoon fine sea salt

⅓ cup coffee liqueur, such as Kahlua (see tips, page 140)

3 tablespoons tapioca flour

2 tablespoons raw macadamia butter (see sidebar, page 16)

1 teaspoon vanilla extract

COCOA COOKIE-CRUMB CRUST

(can be prepared up to 1 day in advance)

¾ cup sorghum flour

¾ cup natural unsweetened cocoa powder

½ cup unrefined cane sugar

2 tablespoons tapioca flour

¾ teaspoon fine sea salt

8 tablespoons vegan buttery spread, melted

1 tablespoon nondairy milk

To make the ice cream, put the coconut milk beverage, canned coconut milk, agave nectar, instant coffee, and salt in a medium saucepan and whisk to combine. Cook over medium-high heat just until the mixture begins to bubble. Put the Kahlua and tapioca flour in a small bowl and whisk until no lumps remain. Add the tapioca flour mixture to the mixture in the saucepan, whisking constantly. Cook over medium heat until the mixture thickens and coats the back of a spoon, about 3 minutes. Remove from the heat.

Put the macadamia butter in a small bowl. Using a ladle, transfer about ¼ cup of the thickened mixture to the bowl and whisk until smooth. Pour the macadamia nut mixture into the saucepan and add the vanilla extract. Whisk until the mixture is smooth; this will be the ice-cream base. Scrape the ice-cream base into a large bowl using a rubber spatula. Let it cool completely at room temperature, then refrigerate for 8 hours.

If you're using an ice-cream maker, follow the manufacturer's instructions. If you're making the ice cream by hand, see page 120. The ice cream should be at the soft-serve stage when the dessert is assembled.

To make the crust, position an oven rack in the middle of the oven. Preheat the oven to 300 degrees F. Line a baking sheet with parchment paper or a Silpat liner. Lightly coat a 9-inch glass pie plate with vegan buttery spread.

Put the sorghum flour, cocoa powder, sugar, tapioca flour, and salt in the bowl of a stand mixer or a large bowl and stir with a dry whisk to combine. Add 6 tablespoons of the buttery spread and the nondairy milk. Turn the stand mixer or a hand mixer on medium-low speed and beat until the mixture starts to come together in small clusters. Using a rubber spatula, spread the

Per slice: 662 calories, 8 g protein, 41 g fat (19 g sat), 74 g carbohydrates, 99 mg sodium, 30 mg calcium, 8 g fiber

CHOCOLATE GANACHE

1¼ cups nondairy semisweet chocolate chips

⅓ cup unsweetened coconut milk beverage

2 teaspoons vegan buttery spread

⅛ teaspoon fine sea salt

FINISHING TOUCHES

⅔ cup chopped almonds, toasted (see sidebar, page 16) **and cooled**

mixture on the prepared baking sheet as thinly as possible. Bake on the middle rack for 22 to 25 minutes. Let cool completely.

Once the mixture has cooled, break it into crumbs and put them in the bowl of the stand mixer or a large bowl. Add the remaining 2 tablespoons of the buttery spread and turn the stand mixer or a hand mixer on medium-low speed until the mixture is well combined. Press the mixture evenly into the bottom and up the sides of the prepared pie plate to form a crust. (If you find it difficult to press the mixture into the dish, simply spread it in the dish and put it in the freezer for 5 minutes. Then press it again—it will be easier to handle.) Put the crust in the freezer.

To make the ganache, use the stove-top method to melt the chocolate (see page 20). Put the chocolate chips, coconut milk beverage, buttery spread, and salt in the bowl over the saucepan. Stir occasionally, until the chocolate is completely melted and the mixture is smooth. Remove from the heat. Let stand for 5 minutes.

To assemble, remove the crust from the freezer. Spread about one-third of the ganache on the crust using a metal offset spatula, reserving the rest for the top of the mud pie (you can leave it at room temperature). Put the crust in the freezer to 30 minutes.

Remove the crust from the freezer and immediately spread the ice cream evenly into the crust using a rubber spatula. Put the mud pie in the freezer for 30 minutes.

After the 30 minutes, the top of the mud pie should be firm; if not, put the mud pie back in the freezer for 20 minutes longer. Spread the remaining ganache on top of the mud pie using a metal offset spatula; if the ganache isn't spreadable, reheat it until it's warm but not hot. The ganache should cover the mud pie but not overflow, so don't try to use up all the ganache. Put the mud pie in the freezer for 10 minutes; the ganache will become firm enough to allow you to top it with the rest. Sprinkle with the almonds. Put the mud pie in the freezer until it's completely firm, at least 4 hours.

To serve, run a knife under hot water and dry it off before using it to slice the mud pie. If the pie is too firm, let it stand at room temperature for about 15 minutes before serving. Store leftovers in the freezer.

TIPS

- Because some instant coffee varieties aren't gluten-free or free of other allergens, I recommend single-serve packets of Starbucks VIA Ready Brew.
- Kahlua is a vegan coffee liqueur that is free of dairy products, eggs, gluten, and soy. If you substitute another coffee liqueur for Kahlua, check with the manufacturer for potential allergens.
- If desired, you can make the crust the day before when you prepare the ice cream; then churn the ice cream, prepare the ganache, and assemble as directed.
- If you're making the ice cream by hand, you can take advantage of the long freezing time by making the crust in between churning times. The crust can be chilled, baked, and cooled by the time the ice cream is at the soft-serve stage. Then prepare the ganache, and assemble as directed.

This pie is inspired by an old family favorite, but this new-and-improved version eliminates refined sugars, highlights good fats, and includes whole grains and fruit. And yet it's still really darned amazing—just like the original.

FROZEN Cocoa-Banana Pie WITH CRISPY PEANUT BUTTER CRUST

FREE OF: SEEDS, YEAST

YIELD: 8 SLICES

CRISPY PEANUT BUTTER CRUST
(can be prepared up to 2 days in advance)

½ cup plus 2 tablespoons natural creamy peanut butter

½ cup agave nectar

3 cups gluten-free crispy brown rice cereal (see tip)

COCOA-BANANA FILLING

3 large bananas, peeled, cut into chunks, and frozen

1 cup mashed avocado flesh (about 2 avocados)

6 tablespoons natural unsweetened cocoa powder

¼ cup agave nectar

1 teaspoon vanilla extract

⅛ teaspoon fine sea salt

PEANUT BUTTER–BANANA TOPPING

1 large banana, peeled, cut into chunks, and frozen

⅓ cup natural creamy peanut butter

1 tablespoon agave nectar

½ teaspoon vanilla extract

⅛ teaspoon fine sea salt

Per slice: 440 calories, 10 g protein, 21 g fat (3 g sat), 55 g carbohydrates, 75 mg sodium, 12 mg calcium, 7 g fiber

To make the crust, put the peanut butter and agave nectar in a small saucepan and cook over medium heat, stirring often, until smooth and thick, about 3 minutes. Put the cereal in a medium bowl and scrape in the peanut butter mixture using a rubber spatula. Stir until well combined, being careful not to crush the cereal. If necessary, use your hands (be careful, the mixture will be hot).

Scrape the mixture into a 10-inch springform pan using the rubber spatula. Using your fingers, press the mixture firmly into the bottom and about one inch up the sides of the pan to form a crust. Put the crust in the freezer while you prepare the filling.

To make the filling, put the bananas, avocado flesh, cocoa powder, agave nectar, vanilla extract, and salt in a food processor and process until smooth. Remove the crust from the freezer and spread the filling evenly into the crust using a rubber spatula, smoothing the top. Put the pie in the freezer for 30 minutes before preparing the topping.

To make the topping, put the banana, peanut butter, agave nectar, vanilla extract, and salt in the food processor and process until smooth. Remove the pie from the freezer. Scrape the topping onto the filling using a rubber spatula and spread the topping evenly over the filling in a thin layer, leaving a 1-inch border. Put the pie in the freezer until the filling has a soft-serve consistency, about 5 hours; for a firmer consistency, leave the pie in the freezer for 12 hours.

To serve, run a knife under hot water and dry it off before using it to slice the pie. If the pie is too firm, let it stand at room temperature for about 15 minutes before serving. Store leftovers in the freezer.

TIP: Some varieties of crispy rice cereal contain barley malt or unnecessary preservatives, such as BHT. I recommend Nature's Path's brand, which contains brown rice (a nutritional bonus!) and is also free of refined sugars and preservatives.

Pineapple, rum-spiked ice cream, coconut, and macadamia nuts are featured in an adults-only frozen cake that will make your taste buds feel like they're vacationing in the tropics. The crust can be prepared one day in advance to make assembly quick and easy (see tips, page 144).

FROZEN PINEAPPLE Upside-Down Cake

FREE OF: PEANUTS, SEEDS, YEAST

YIELD: 10 SLICES

RUM ICE CREAM

1¼ cups unsweetened coconut milk beverage

1 (14-ounce) **can full-fat coconut milk**

½ cup agave nectar

¼ teaspoon fine sea salt

¼ cup white rum (see tips, page 144)

3 tablespoons tapioca flour

2 tablespoons raw macadamia butter (see sidebar, page 16)

CARAMELIZED PINEAPPLE TOPPING

1 small pineapple, peeled and cored

3 tablespoons agave nectar

2 tablespoons vegan buttery spread

¼ teaspoon vanilla extract

Pinch fine sea salt

To make the ice cream, put the coconut milk beverage, canned coconut milk, agave nectar, and salt in a medium saucepan and whisk to combine. Cook over medium-high heat just until the mixture begins to bubble. Put the rum and tapioca flour in a small bowl and whisk until no lumps remain. Add the tapioca flour mixture to the mixture in the saucepan, whisking constantly. Cook over medium heat, stirring occasionally, until the mixture thickens and coats the back of a spoon, about 3 minutes. Remove from the heat.

Put the macadamia butter in a small bowl. Using a ladle, transfer about ¼ cup of the thickened mixture to the bowl and whisk until smooth. Pour the macadamia butter mixture into the saucepan. Whisk until the mixture is smooth; this will be the ice-cream base. Scrape the ice-cream base into a large bowl using a rubber spatula. Let it cool completely at room temperature, then refrigerate for 8 hours.

If you're using an ice-cream maker, follow the manufacturer's instructions. If you're making the ice cream by hand, see page 120. The ice cream should be at the soft-serve stage when the dessert is assembled.

To make the topping, cover the bottom and sides of a 10-inch round springform pan with aluminum foil. Cut the pineapple into 1½-inch squares about ¼ inch thick. Put the pineapple, agave nectar, and buttery spread in a medium skillet over medium heat and cook, stirring often, until the pineapple starts to turn golden and browns on the edges, 13 to 16 minutes. Remove from the heat. Stir in the vanilla extract and salt until well combined. Scrape the mixture into the prepared pan using a rubber spatula, spreading it into an even layer. Refrigerate until you're ready to assemble the dessert.

Per slice: 441 calories, 3 g protein, 30 g fat (14 g sat), 41 g carbohydrates, 118 mg sodium, 15 mg calcium, 3 g fiber

COCONUT-MACADAMIA CRUMB CRUST

⅔ cup dry-roasted salted macadamia nuts

¾ cup unsweetened finely shredded dried coconut

6 tablespoons sorghum flour

¼ cup unrefined cane sugar

2 tablespoons tapioca flour

¼ teaspoon fine sea salt

¼ cup plus 2 tablespoons vegan buttery spread, melted

1 tablespoon nondairy milk

1 tablespoon agave nectar

To make the crumb crust, position an oven rack in the middle of the oven. Preheat the oven to 300 degrees F. Line a baking sheet with parchment paper or a Silpat liner.

Put the macadamia nuts in a food processor and pulse until the macadamia nuts are coarsely ground. Transfer the nuts to the bowl of a stand mixer or a large bowl. Add the dried coconut, sorghum flour, sugar, tapioca flour, and salt and stir with a dry whisk until well combined. Add ¼ cup of the buttery spread and the nondairy milk. Turn the stand mixer or a hand mixer on medium-low speed and beat until the mixture starts to come together in small clusters. Using a rubber spatula, spread the mixture on the prepared baking sheet as thinly as possible. Bake on the middle rack for 23 to 25 minutes, until the clusters feel dry to the touch. Let cool completely. Break up the clusters and put the crumbs in a large bowl. Cover with a lid or plastic wrap until you're ready to assemble the dessert.

To assemble, put the topping in the freezer for 1 hour. Remove the topping from the freezer and immediately spread the ice cream evenly over the topping using a rubber spatula. Put the cake in the freezer for 15 minutes. The ice cream should be firm enough to top with the crust mixture; if not, put the cake back in the freezer for 10 minutes longer.

Add the remaining 2 tablespoons of melted buttery spread and the agave nectar to the crust mixture and stir until well combined. Sprinkle the crumb crust evenly over the ice cream. Press down lightly, just enough to push the crust into the ice cream. The crust will be sticky so put the cake back in the freezer for 5 minutes, then lightly press the crust into the ice cream again. It should stick without crumbling. Put the cake in the freezer until it's completely firm, at least 4 hours.

To serve, run a knife under hot water and dry it off before using it to slice the cake. If the cake is too firm, let it stand at room temperature for about 15 minutes before serving. Store leftovers in the freezer.

TIPS

- Most white rum is vegan and free of dairy products, eggs, gluten, and soy. Check with the manufacturer for potential allergens.
- If desired, the topping and crumb crust can be prepared the day before. When preparing the crust crumbs, don't add the additional buttery spread or agave nectar; instead, add those ingredients to the crust right before you assemble the dessert.
- If you prepare the topping and crust the day of assembly, make sure both are completely cooled before assembling the dessert.
- If you're making the ice cream by hand, you can take advantage of the long freezing time by making the topping and crumb crust in between churning times. Both will be cooled by the time the ice cream is at the soft-serve stage. Then finish the crust, and assemble as directed.

Conversions

The following tables provide information to help you make conversions if necessary. This book uses conventional measures, which are listed in table 6, page 146. Metric equivalents can be found in table 7, page 146. Before making substitutions, keep these points in mind:

- To measure the depth of a pan, measure the middle of the pan.
- To measure the length and width of a pan, measure from the inside edges.
- To measure the volume of a pan, use a measuring cup to fill the pan to the brim with water. The volume of the pan is equal to the amount of water required to fill it.
- When using dark baking pans or glass baking dishes instead of light-colored metal pans, decrease the oven temperature by 25 degrees F.
- Food will bake more quickly in a larger pan, so decrease the baking time accordingly.

TABLE 6 Conventional pan sizes, capacity, and substitutions

Pan	Capacity	Substitutions
1 (9-inch) round pan	6 cups	1 (8-inch) round pan 1 (8 x 4-inch) loaf pan 1 (11 x 7-inch) baking dish
1 (8-inch square) baking dish	8 cups	1 (9 x 2-inch) deep-dish pie plate 1 (9 x 5-inch) loaf pan 2 (8-inch) pie plates
1 (9-inch square) baking dish	8 cups	1 (9 x 2-inch) deep-dish pie plate 1 (9 x 5-inch) loaf pan 1 (11 x 7-inch) baking dish 2 (8-inch) pie plates
1 (9-inch) springform pan	10 cups	1 (10-inch) round pan 1 (10-inch) springform pan 2 (8-inch) round pans 2 (9-inch) round pans
1 (10-inch) springform pan	12 cups	1 (9-inch) tube pan 1 (10-inch) Bundt pan 2 (8-inch) round pans 2 (8 x 4-inch) loaf pans 2 (9-inch) round pans 2 (11 x 7-inch) baking dishes
2 (9-inch) round pans	12 cups	1 (9-inch) tube pan 1 (10-inch) Bundt pan 1 (10-inch) springform pan 2 (8-inch) round pans 2 (8 x 4-inch) loaf pans 2 (11 x 7-inch) baking dishes

TABLE 7 Pan sizes (conventional and metric)

Pan	Metric measure (centimeters)
8 x 8-inch square	20 x 20-centimeter square
9 x 2-inch round	22 x 5-centimeter round
9 x 9-inch square	22 x 22-centimeter square

About the Author

Laurie Sadowski's love of food began with her first bite of rice Pablum. At a young age, she was introduced to fruit trees and vegetable gardens, and she later became a food writer and restaurant reviewer. Her creativity in the kitchen began when she was diagnosed with celiac disease. Soon after, she self-published a gluten-free, casein-free cookbook, *Mission in the Kitchen*.

The adoption of a vegan diet further fueled Laurie's foodie fire. After winning the vegetarian category in a national recipe competition and cook-off, she became a vegan food columnist for her local newspaper. Her love of food and health, combined with a passion for helping others, drove her to write a series of gluten-free cookbooks that also addressed other common food allergies. *The Allergy-Free Cook Bakes Bread* was first, and *The Allergy-Free Cook Bakes Cakes and Cookies* soon followed. *The Allergy-Free Cook Bakes Pies and Desserts* is the third installment.

Laurie lives in the Niagara region of Ontario, Canada, where she promotes healthful living, cooks and bakes, and continues her studies in music and art. And, you know, constantly dreams about food.

Index

Q

R

S

T

U

V

W

X

Y

books that educate, inspire, and empower

To find your favorite vegetarian products online, visit:
healthy-eating.com

The Allergy-Free Cook Bakes Bread
Laurie Sadowski
978-1-57067-262-0 • $14.95

The Allergy-Free Cook
Bakes Cakes and Cookies
Laurie Sadowski
978-1-57067-291-0 • $14.95

Simple Treats
Ellen Abraham
978-1-57067-137-1 • $14.95

Gluten-Free Gourmet
Desserts and Baked Goods
Valerie Cupillard
978-1-57067-187-6 • $24.95

Quinoa
Beth Geisler
with recipes by Jo Stepaniak
978-1-55312-050-6 • $11.95

Food Allergy Survival Guide
Vesanto Melina, RD,
Jo Stepaniak, MSEd, and
Dina Aronson, RD
978-1-57067-163-0 • $19.95

Purchase these health titles and cookbooks from your local bookstore or natural food store,
or you can buy them directly from:

Book Publishing Company • P.O. Box 99 • Summertown, TN 38483 • 1-800-695-2241

Please include $3.95 per book for shipping and handling.